MUSIC BULLETIN BOARDS
ACTIVITIES KIT

MUSIC BULLETIN BOARDS ACTIVITIES KIT

Year-Round Displays for the Music Classroom

Nancy Forquer
Marjorie Partin

PARKER PUBLISHING COMPANY
West Nyack, New York 10995

Library of Congress Cataloging-in-Publication Data

Forquer, Nancy E., [date]
    Music bulletin boards activities kit : year-round displays for the
music classroom / Nancy Forquer and Marjorie Partin.
        p.   cm.
    Bibliography: p.
    ISBN 0-13-606898-7
    1. School music—Instruction and study.   2. Bulletin boards—
Handbooks, manuals, etc.   I. Partin, Marjorie, [date].
II. Title.
MT1.F712   1989
780′.7—dc20   89-16321
                                                                    CIP
                                                                    MN

© 1990 *by*
PARKER PUBLISHING COMPANY
West Nyack, New York

10   9   8   7   6   5   4   3   2   1

ISBN 0-13-606898-7

PARKER PUBLISHING COMPANY
BUSINESS & PROFESSIONAL DIVISION
A division of Simon & Schuster
West Nyack, New York 10995

Printed in the United States of America

In memory of James Robert Partin

We would like to thank Linda Ellis, a dear friend, for her inspiration and encouragement. Her many comments about the bulletin boards resulted in this book. Thanks, Linda . . . and thanks to Karen, too.

ABOUT THE AUTHORS

NANCY FORQUER received her bachelor's and master's degrees from Northeast Missouri State University. Currently an elementary music teacher with the Macon, Missouri RI schools, she has over seventeen years of experience as a music educator and has served as clinician for various state music conferences. Mrs. Forquer is also the author of *Elementary Teacher's Complete Handbook of Music Activities* (Parker Publishing Company, 1979), as well as two Christmas musicals, "Trial of the Christmas Bells" and "Substitute Santa."

MARJORIE PARTIN received her bachelor's and master's degrees from Northeast Missouri State University. Now retired, she taught art for twenty-four years in the Kirksville, Missouri and Trenton, Missouri school systems.

ABOUT THIS KIT

The *Music Bulletin Boards Activities Kit* is for all music teachers of grades 1–6 who want to display attractive and educational bulletin boards, but who do not have the time to create original designs. In this book you'll find nineteen bulletin boards plus over 150 activities that will help motivate your students throughout the school year.

Complete, easy-to-follow construction directions, as well as any patterns that may be needed, are given for each bulletin board. Following each bulletin board is a unit complete with lesson activities, reproducible worksheets, and answer keys. The activities progress from easy to more advanced materials so that you may select the ones best suited to your students. For example, some upper-grade students who meet only once a week may require easier material, while lower elementary classes that meet every day might use more advanced activities.

The *Kit* offers an organized approach to teaching music in grades 1–6. Not only are the bulletin boards seasonal and colorful, they are also sequential and offer all major concepts that must be taught throughout the year. For example:

- September's "Blasting Off to a Good Year" bulletin board improves students' singing abilities by introducing them to ten good singing habits. Some of the activities include "Tempo," "Move with Scarves," and "How Many Phrases?"

- November's "Missing Mystery Instrument" bulletin board introduces students to musical instruments. You'll find such activities as "Instruments Around the Room," "Sound Composition," and "Instrument Crossword Puzzle" to help your students become familiar with various instruments.

- January's "Chugging Into the New Year" display improves students' knowledge of dynamics. Students will apply dynamic markings to actual song material in such activities as "Listening and Labeling Dynamics," "Playing with Dynamics," and "Loud or Soft?"

- March's "The Tempo Trail" bulletin board introduces students to the tempo markings of *presto, moderato,* and *andante.* The activities include "Moving to Tempo," "Using the Metronome," and "Tempo Wordsearch."

- April's "Showers of Scales" display increases the students' understanding of major, pentatonic, and chromatic scales. Some of the activities are "Pentatonic Accompaniment," "Sharps and Flats," and "Building Chords from Scales."

- June's "It's Been a Long Year, but the End Is in Sight" bulletin board provides a review of all the concepts learned during the school year. Review tests are included for each unit in the book, including music history, folk music, and rhythms and rests.

So, you can see that using the *Music Bulletin Boards Activities Kit* will help you teach musical concepts easily as the entire school year unfolds. The bulletin boards will visually motivate your students as they have fun learning the integrated musical information. Enjoy!

Nancy Forquer
Marjorie Partin

CONTENTS

OCTOBER   29

NOVEMBER 55

MISSING MYSTERY INSTRUMENT: Bulletin Board   56

Objective
Materials Needed
Construction Directions
Unit Activities

TURKEY TUNES: Bulletin Board   67

Objective
Materials Needed
Construction Directions
Unit Activities

DECEMBER 83

ELVES AND ELEMENTS: Bulletin Board   84

STAR SEARCH: Bulletin Board   96

JANUARY 107

FEBRUARY 133

MARCH   163

LEARNING NOTES WITH THE LAZY LEPRECHAUN: Bulletin Board   164

𝄞PRIL   181

MAY   205

JUNE 219

September

"Blasting Off to a Good Year"

"Let's 'Fall' for Music History"

BLASTING OFF TO A GOOD YEAR: The Bulletin Board

Objective: Students will improve their singing ability by observing good singing habits.

Materials Needed:

Blue background paper
Construction paper (grey, orange, yellow, and dark blue)
Black felt-tip pens
Silver paper or foil
Scissors
Glue
Straight pins

Construction Directions:

1. Use an opaque projector or transparency for tracing. It is also possible to photocopy the patterns and letters. Put these copies into a thermofax so the resulting transparencies can be used on an overhead projector for tracing.
   a. Trace the lettering on background paper. (Simple block letters may be cut from construction paper if desired.)
   b. Trace and cut the center smoke shape on grey construction paper and the small flame on orange paper.
   c. Trace and cut the moon and outside rocket flame on yellow construction paper.

2. To make the rocket, fold the top corners of the red construction paper rectangle to make a pointed top, as shown here. Then, glue the back to make the rocket shape as shown. This will give a three-dimensional effect. Decorate with silver.

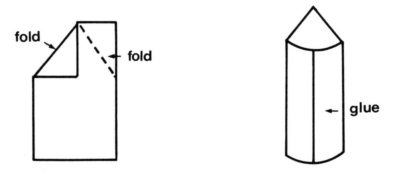

3. For the rocket's fins, fold the dark blue construction paper in half. Then fold the top corners to the center fold, as shown here. (You will need two of these.)

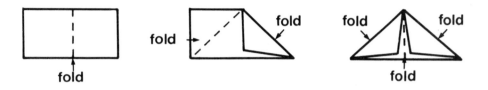

4. Make ten yellow construction paper stars using smaller star patterns. (Use black felt-tip pen for lettering.)

5. Make ten silver stars using larger star patterns.

6. Use straight pins to attach the rocket to the background in the center of the board under the lettering. Attach the fins and smoke with straight pins.

7. Arrange the moon and yellow and silver stars on each side of the rocket.

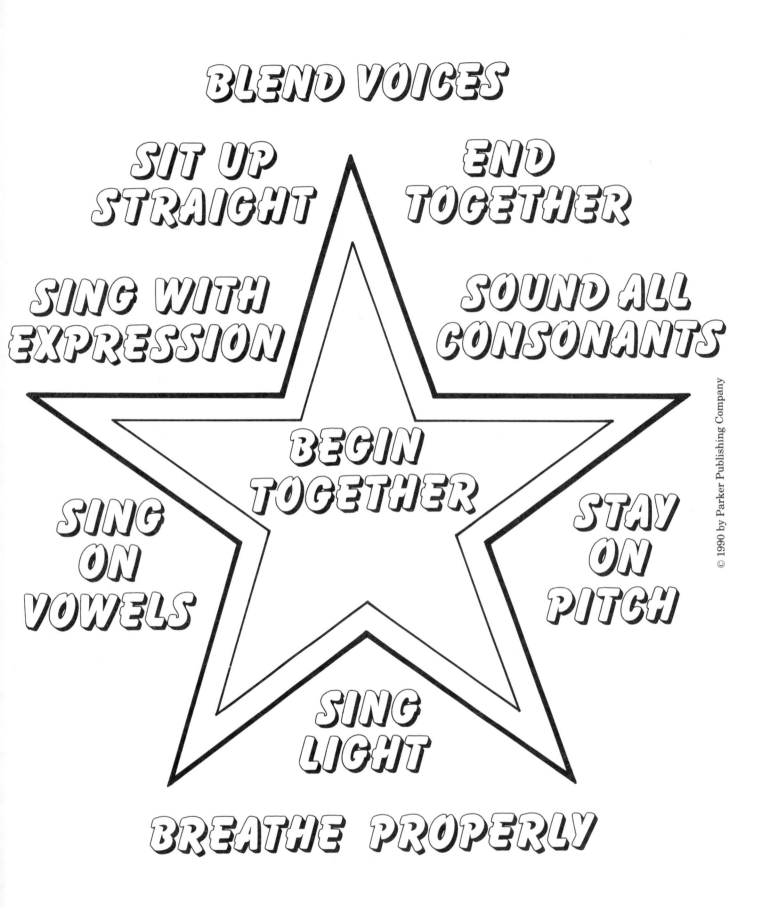

BLASTING OFF TO A GOOD YEAR

BLASTING OFF TO A GOOD YEAR: Unit Activities

It is important to "Blast Off to a Good Year" in music. The stars in this bulletin board could represent various aspects of the coming year. They could contain units to be studied during the year, conduct rules, information on the first unit to be studied, or goals for the year. This is also the right time to focus on good singing habits to be established for all singing activities during the year. The following games and activities help to make students aware of the good singing habits that are so important to a polished performance. All the poems at the beginning of each activity are sung to the tune of "Are You Sleeping." They will help students remember each of the good singing habits. The "poem-songs" will help students in early grades to focus on good singing habits. Gradually through the years more information should be given, additional diagrams studied, reports presented and harder exercises practiced as indicated in the lessons that follow. This assures proper attention to good singing habits throughout the grades. By junior high all information in this unit should have been presented. The teacher may begin the board with one star; as each new singing habit is discussed and sung another star can be added by a student. The teacher may sing a song and omit a good singing habit. Have students come to the board and point to the habit that was not performed properly.

SIT UP STRAIGHT

Sit up straight. Sit up straight.
Raise your chest. Raise your chest.
Always have good posture. Always have good posture.
Look your best. Look your best.

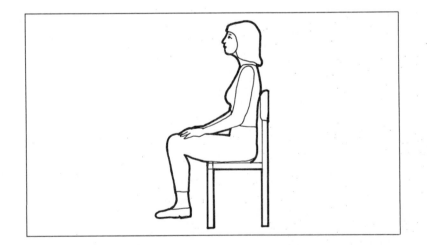

SEATED: Both feet should be on the floor with the back straight and away from the chair's back. The chest should be up and the shoulders pulled back in line with the hips.

The first step in producing a good singing tone is proper standing or sitting position. Help students realize that it isn't only for appearance that they should sit up straight. Proper posture is essential to produce the correct sound. Discuss the following illustrations and explanations for posture with your students.

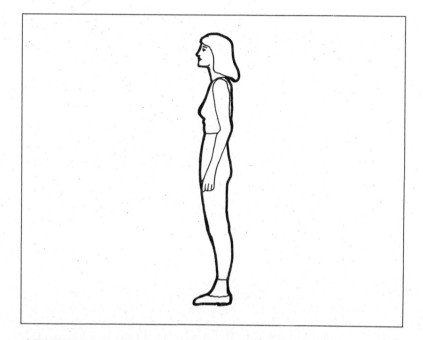

STANDING: The feet should be several inches apart with the weight on the balls of the feet. The chest should be raised with the spine straight and the shoulders pulled back in line with the hips.

Show students how sitting up straight allows air into the diaphragm for a better sound. (See the activities listed under "Breathe Properly.") It is also beneficial to assign a student to give a report on breathing and sound production.

Make a game of "catching" students who are not sitting straight. While singing, watch to see students who are not sitting properly. Write the student's name on the chalkboard and that student is then out of the game.

BEGIN TOGETHER

> Start together. Start together.
> Don't hesitate. Don't hesitate.
> Sing the very first note. Sing the very first note.
> Don't be late. Don't be late.

Students should realize from their earliest singing experiences that it is important to begin together. Any time an "attack" is not good, have students start again. This will stress the importance of beginning songs together with a good, solid sound. This concept can also be stressed through the following activities.

Put the Music Inside

Write four lines of rhythms on the chalkboard. Ask students to "put the last line inside" and see if they can start together again on the first line. Repeat the exercise at least three times. In upper grades the rhythms should be longer and more difficult. Here are some sample rhythms:

Sing the Phrase

Choose any familiar song and ask students to sing various phrases, such as 1, 2, and 4; 1 and 3; 1, 3, and 4; or 1 and 4. Students should begin together every time they begin a new phrase. For example, try using "Skip to My Lou."

1. Skip, skip, skip to my Lou
2. Skip, skip, skip to my Lou
3. Skip, skip, skip to my Lou
4. Skip to my Lou my darling

Watch the Director

Choose any familiar song so students do not have to watch the music as they watch you direct. Cut off at various times during the song and bring them in again later in the song. At first, begin and end only after complete phrases. Later, make it more difficult by cutting off in the middle of phrases and beginning in the middle of a phrase.

Begin After Introduction

Play the introductions to various familiar songs so students can try to begin together. Have a list of five familiar songs and go directly from one to another with only an introduction between each. For example:

1. "Twinkle, Twinkle Little Star"
2. "Are You Sleeping?"
3. "Skip to My Lou"
4. "John Brown"
5. "She'll Be Coming 'Round the Mountain"

BREATHE PROPERLY

> Take a big breath. Take a big breath.
> Get enough air. Get enough air.
> You will have a better sound. You will have a better sound.
> Just compare. Just compare.

The following illustrations should be shown to students, with an explanation of proper breathing. If the process of breathing has been thoroughly explained with diagrams and charts, you will only have to say "Remember to breathe correctly" and students will understand the process. To produce a full tone quality, it is necessary for students to breathe correctly. Breathing or respiration involves two parts, inhaling and exhaling.

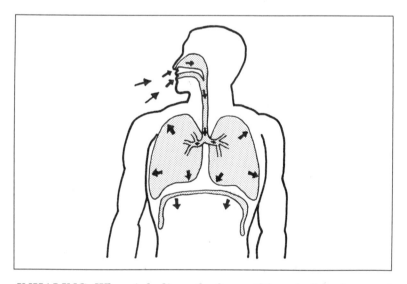

INHALING: When inhaling, the lungs (like a bellows) expand to take in air. The diaphragm is flattened and the ribs move outward.

Breathing Exercise 1: Place hands gently on front of body, just above the waist. Inhale and exhale slowly. Notice your hands moving out as you inhale and in as you exhale.

Breathing Exercise 2: Place hands on each side of the body. Inhale on eight counts. Hold your breath for eight counts and exhale on eight counts. Again notice how the hands move out as you inhale and in as you exhale.

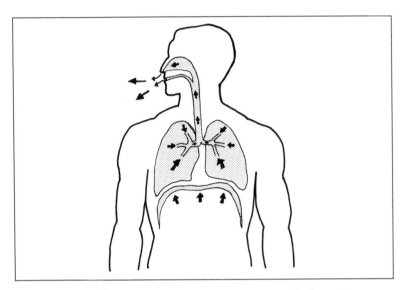

EXHALING: When exhaling, the lungs are deflated because the air is breathed out. The diaphragm returns to its position, and the rib muscles relax.

Breathing Exercise 3: Take a deep breath and exhale on eight counts with a hissing sound ("sssss . . .").

Breathing Exercise 4: Take a deep breath and sing the following vowels. Sing on each note of the scale.

a - ee - ah - o - oo

BLEND VOICES

Blend your voices. Blend your voices.
Unity. Unity.
Sound like one together. Sound like one together.
Try it and see. Try it and see.

Any time students are getting a "good" blend with their voices, compliment them. Tell them to sing again and to listen as they sing so that they can hear how a good blend should sound and feel. If students are getting a "bad" blend, stop them and work on their blend and tone. Describe a good blend by saying, "Everyone should sound like one voice. If your voices are blended together, I should not hear any one voice above the others. All thirty voices should blend so well that it sounds like one voice."

Work with numbers to blend voices. This isolates the problems so students don't have to handle song material as well as blending voices. Start with two groups on "five" (Sol) and "three" (Mi). Use other numbers in two groups, such as "one" (Do) and "five" (Sol); "four" (Fa) and "six" (La); etc. When students are able to blend two parts together, advance to three parts. Sing various chords as follows:

Always start with the low note and add the upper notes as the low notes are held. Stop and start again when the blend is not good.

Listen to recordings of choral groups and critique them. Bring in examples with good blend so that the students can hear the proper sound.

Record the class at various times. Replay examples of both good and bad blends so that the students can compare.

SING LIGHTLY

Sing out softly. Sing out softly.

Make it light. Make it light.

Always sing a pretty tone. Always sing a pretty tone.

Sound just right. Sound just right.

Never allow students to use a "shouting" tone while singing. Often students will sing very loudly on their favorite songs. They somehow feel louder is better. Stop and begin songs again when loud, harsh singing is heard. Help students realize that a light tone is more beautiful than loud, boisterous singing. Work on light singing with echoes. Ask students to "Make your voice sound like mine," "Make a light beautiful sound," or "Listen as you sing and make sure we have a pretty sound, not a loud ugly sound." Sing with echoes on numbers or syllables as follows:

(teacher)   (student)

Echoes can become more difficult as students progress. The light singing tone achieved through the echoes should be carried over into the singing of song material. Recording the class for critique and playing tapes or records of quality singing groups can also help students achieve a good, light singing tone.

SING ON VOWELS

> Sing on vowels. Sing on vowels.
> A, E, I—O and U.
> You will have a better sound. You will have a better sound.
> If you do. If you do.

Ask students to sustain or hold a note on a consonant (*D, P, F, T,* or *H,* for example). They will find this task difficult. Explain that we can only hold notes on vowels and that it is impossible to hold a note on a consonant. Do the following exercises to stress singing on vowels. Sing exercises on each note of the scale.

Choose a song that the students are performing. Go over it word by word, stressing and exaggerating the vowel sounds. Sing the song and concentrate on singing the vowel sounds correctly.

SOUND ALL CONSONANTS

> Sound all consonants. Sound all consonants.
> Make words clear. Make words clear.
> Help to understand you. Help to understand you.
> All who hear. All who hear.

In order to be understood, it is important that articulation of consonants be precise. All beginning and ending consonants must be sounded together. Do the following exercises to stress sounding consonants.

lah - la - lee - lo - loo,   tah - ta - tee - to - too,   kah - ka - kee - ko - koo

Sing this exercise using various consonant sounds. Practice the exercise on each note of the scale to increase range.

dah — may — nee — po — too — lah — bay —

Sing this exercise on each note of the scale. Start the exercise slowly and increase speed as students become familiar with it. This will help students "spit out" consonant sounds quickly and accurately.

Choose another familiar song and again go over it word by word, exaggerating the consonant sounds. Students should end all "t," "s," "b," etc., sounds together at the end of words. Record the song to let students hear if they are sounding all consonants.

STAY ON PITCH

> Stay on pitch. Stay on pitch.
> Don't slide low. Don't slide low.
> Hit the note exactly. Hit the note exactly.
> Not below. Not below.

Even young students should be aware that they must "get their voices in the right place." Echo syllables or numbers as a group to let the students concentrate on staying on pitch. Later, do this individually and keep records of those students unable to stay on pitch. Try to work with them individually at a later time. Use phrases like "Make your voice high as if you were afraid," "Pretend you are a monster and start low on oooooh . . . , then go high on oooooh . . . . ," or "Listen before you try to sing."

Divide the class into two groups. Sing syllables or number patterns that individual students must repeat. Those who are wrong must sit down as in an old-fashioned spelling bee. The side with the most people standing at the end of a time period is the winner. Echo examples should be progressively harder. Some simple beginning echoes might be as follows. You are to sing the patterns and have the students repeat them on the rests.

5   4   3   3   2   1   1   3   5   5   5   1
Sol Fa Mi   Mi Re Do   Do Mi Sol   Sol Sol Do

SING WITH EXPRESSION

> Sing with expression. Sing with expression.
> Feel the phrase. Feel the phrase.
> Watching all the markings. Watching all the markings.
> Will earn you praise. Will earn you praise.

Singing with expression can include many facets of music. Activities included in the following lessons focus on phrasing, dynamics, and tempo. Observing these elements in music achieves an expressive performance.

Phrasing

Explain to your students, "A phrase is where you feel like pausing or stopping in the music. It is like a sentence. You feel that you are at the end of one thought and ready to begin another thought."

How Many Phrases?

Play various songs and have students state how many phrases are in the song. At first, use songs with words to help students determine phrasing. Later, play music without words to see if students can state how many phrases are in the song. Also, use this technique in listening lessons of classical recordings.

Move with Scarves

Students should feel phrasing as well as understand it. Explain that a phrase moves along to a climax and then comes to an end as the musical idea is completed. Give several students scarves and ask them to move to the music with their scarves to show the phrasing. As students move, you should point out those students who are moving to the music very well. "Johnny is moving very fast, just as the phrase is." "Susan has come to an end, just as the phrase has." "Look at Jean. Her movements are slow and smooth just like the phrase."

Dynamics

Get two sheets of 8½″ × 11″ construction paper and, using a marker, write *p* on one sheet and *f* on the other. Ask students to explain what *p* and *f* mean in music. Usually a piano student will know. Ask students, "Why don't we use *s* for 'soft' and *l* for 'loud'?" Then explain, "Music began long ago in Italy before the United

States was even a nation. They used Italian words to give directions in music, and we still use those same Italian terms today. So, *p* stands for *piano* in Italian and means 'soft'; *f* stands for *forte* in Italian and means 'loud.' Because music notation began in Italy, we still use the Italian terms today."

Have a student stand before the class with the *p* and *f* sheets. As a familiar song is sung, the students should watch the student with the sheets and sing loudly or softly according to the sheet shown by the student. It may change from *p* to *f* as many times as the student wishes during the song, but the student should not change so fast that the other students don't have time to make the adjustment from loud to soft or soft to loud. As the students progress, add more dynamic markings (*mp, pp, mf, ff*).

Tempo

Before introducing the term "tempo," play a phrase two times—once fast, the next time more slowly. Ask students if the second phrase is faster or slower. After students have done several examples, tell them that the word used to describe fast and slow in music is *tempo*. Play several short songs at various speeds on the piano or on a recording. Have students state whether they are fast, slow, or in-between. Sing a familiar song at various tempos. Have students decide which tempo they like best. Use different kinds of songs, such as a lullaby, a march, a hymn, and a pop song. Students should realize that the words and music work together so the music "feels better" at a certain tempo.

Now introduce the words "accelerando" and "ritardando." Practice a song that is familiar to the class so they can watch you direct. Decide on places in the song where you will accelerate and slow down. Sing the song following all tempo markings.

END TOGETHER

> End together. End together.
> Don't be late. Don't be late.
> Cut off all at one time. Cut off all at one time.
> Sound just great. Sound just great.

During their earliest experiences in music, students should learn the importance of beginning and ending together. Primary music activities usually begin with echo clapping. This is a good place to stress beginning and ending together. It seems to be harder for children to end together than to begin together. When a four-count clapping echo is repeated by the class, usually three or four students will not stop with the rest of the class. Have students repeat the pattern until they end together. Be "very disappointed" when there are a few students who do not end together; praise the class a great deal when the task is done correctly. Simple echo clapping might be as follows. You should clap the rhythm and then wait for the students to echo the rhythm.

♩ ♩ ♫♩___ ♫♩ ♩ ♩___ ♩ ♫♫♩___

Next, try holding a note out at the end of a song and have students watch you direct the cut-off to get it together. Usually first experiences will find a few students shouting as they cut the sound off. Explain that the sound should end together at the same dynamic level, and ask them not to suddenly get louder as they cut off. Practice until they are successful, and make sure the learning carries over in all their song material.

LET'S "FALL" FOR MUSIC HISTORY: The Bulletin Board

Objective: Students will improve their knowledge of music history by listening to recordings and studying various composers and forms of music.

Materials Needed:

   Light blue background paper
   Brown construction paper or butcher wrap
   Construction paper in assorted fall colors
   Black felt-tip pen
   Scissors
   Straight pins

Construction Directions:

   1. Use an opaque projector or transparency to trace the lettering onto the background paper.

   2. Use the opaque projector or transparency to trace the tree onto brown paper. Use a black felt-tip pen to trace the lettering of music periods onto the branches. Attach the tree to the background with straight pins.

   3. Trace the leaf pattern onto appropriate fall leaf colors. Make thirty-seven leaves in all. Use a black felt-tip pen to trace the lettering onto the leaves. Cut out the leaves and attach them to the branches with straight pins. Pull away the paper from the board to give a three-dimensional effect. (NOTE: The leaf pattern shown on the next page has been labeled "Madrigal" to show how each completed leaf should look.)

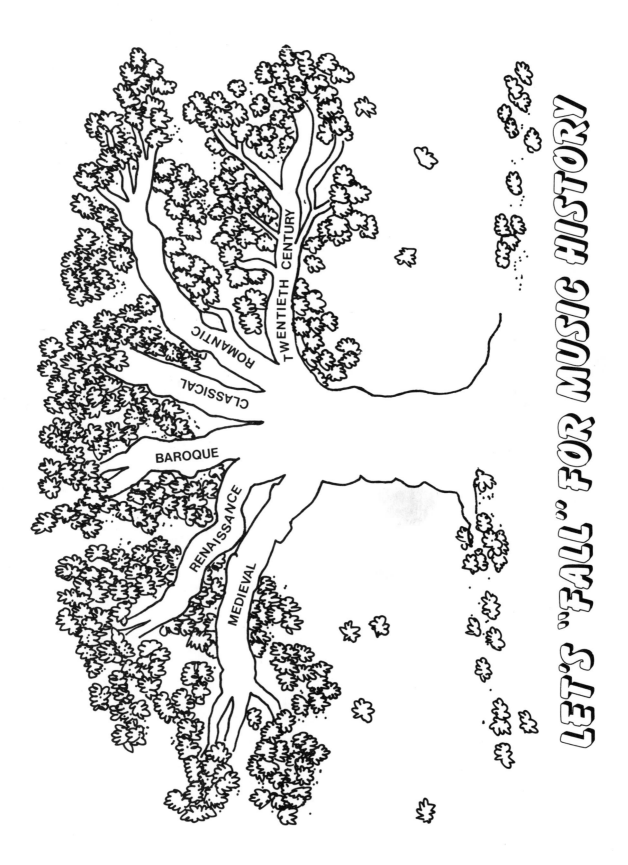

TWENTIETH CENTURY

ROMANTIC

CLASSICAL

BAROQUE

RENAISSANCE

MEDIEVAL

LET'S "FALL" FOR MUSIC HISTORY

LET'S "FALL" FOR MUSIC HISTORY: Unit Activities

This bulletin board provides an excellent guide for the study of music history, literature, forms, and composers. It can be used as a model for setting up listening lessons for the entire year. Upper grades should study history, the sequence and development of form, and composers through listening lessons. Lower grades enjoy listening to stories about composers and their lives. Information concerning composers and forms can be chosen from the following "stories." The teacher should use these "stories" as a reference and choose how much information to give the class according to grade level and ability of the class. Each "story" is presented to help students relate to the development of music history and literature. Older students should seek additional information in the form of reports, films, essays, or scrapbooks. The teacher should point out that although forms are listed under various periods, there is some overlap. Variations, symphonies, and operas are still being written today. Each form is presented in the period of music history in which it was very popular, but many forms continued to be used in other periods through the present. This bulletin board could be moved to a wall and left there the entire year. It would be an excellent reference to help students grasp the concept of the development of music. It is possible to gradually build the bulletin board as each composer or form is studied. Have a student put a leaf on the appropriate branch of the tree as it is studied. Also, play a composition that has previously been studied and ask a student to go to the board and point to the leaf showing the form and composer.

THE MEDIEVAL PERIOD (500–1450)

Medieval times (or the Middle Ages) were those of castles, kings, queens, princes, lords, and ladies. People of that time were either very rich and lived in castles or fine homes, or they were very poor and worked as serfs and slaves. The instruments of this time were simple recorders, lutes (an instrument similar to a guitar), harp-like instruments, and drums. There was no TV, radio, or stereo, and distances between villages and castles were very far. Entertainment was an evening of live performance of singing and dancing.

Church Music

Masses and other forms of church music were sung in choir lofts of the huge and beautiful cathedrals of Europe. The choir members lived in the church and their full-time job was singing in the choir. Only males were allowed to sing, so when high parts were needed they used young boys whose voices had not changed yet. These boys left home at an early age and lived at the church, attending choir school. Only a few boys were chosen, because it took a great deal of talent to qualify. All Masses were sung in Latin, which was the official language of the church. There were not any printing presses in medieval times, so all the music had to be copied by hand. It was the custom to draw elaborate drawings around the music to decorate the page. Notation was very different from ours of today, and it takes special people called "musicologists" to study and figure out how to read the old Masses. Most of the time, people sang *a cappella* (without instrumental accompaniment).

Chanson

Chanson is the French word for song. Troubadours and trouvères originated in France, and they often sang *chansons* to their audiences. These songs were about love, war, adventure, and nature. They were not written down. Since all copying had to be done by hand, only church music was considered important enough to be copied. People in the Middle Ages passed the *chansons* down from generation to generation by listening and singing. These songs are actually a type of folk music, and there may be many versions of one song.

Madrigal

Madrigals were songs that originated in Italy during the Middle Ages. They were popular songs sung by wealthy men and women who often got together after dinner. The groups could be small—made up of only four or five people—or could contain up to twenty or thirty people. The madrigal was one of the first types of songs to contain verses and a refrain as our modern songs do. Madrigals were polyphonic and often sung in four to six parts. Singing was not only a means of entertainment in the Middle Ages, it was also a form of education. Everyone in the castle gathered in the evening to listen to troubadours and trouvères. Afterwards they joined together to sing madrigals. These songs were usually performed *a cappella* and were most often passed on by word-of-mouth, but many were written down so we can enjoy singing them today.

Troubadours and Trouvères

The troubadours and trouvères were traveling musicians who went from castle to castle performing their songs. Sometimes they were just passing through and stayed only one night; other times they spent several months at the same castle. In the evening, everyone in the castle would gather and listen to the troubadours or trouvères. They accompanied themselves on lutes, drums, harps, and other instruments. Usually they sang songs of love, war, adventure, or nature. This was one of the first forms of "pop" music.

Guido d'Arezzo (990–1050)

Guido d'Arezzo was a monk during the Middle Ages. He directed the choir in the large cathedral. There were no printing presses, so all music was written by hand. It was difficult to teach new songs to the choir members. Guido invented a system of syllables to teach songs to his choir members. We still use this system today.

Guillaume Dufay (1400–1474)

Guillaume Dufay was a choirboy at Cambrai. He began singing in the choir when he was nine years old and continued until he was fourteen years old. He studied hard while he was a choir boy and eventually became a great composer. Dufay worked with the old styles of the Middle Ages, but he was one of the first to use the new style with additional harmony and polyphony.

THE RENAISSANCE (1450–1600)

Renaissance means "rebirth," and the Renaissance was a time of learning, exploration, and new ideas. It was still a time of castles, kings, and queens, but it was also a time when humanism and the common man became important. There were not only the very rich and the very poor, but there was also the beginning of a middle class. A new spirit grew, and the arts flourished. One of the most important events that ushered in this new age was the invention of printing with moveable type around 1450. Books could be printed easily so that more learning could take place.

Variation

A *variation* is based on a theme or tune for the entire composition. As the composition is developed, the theme is changed in various ways. Sometimes it is changed very little; other times it is impossible to recognize the theme. Some of the ways the theme can be changed are:

Melody—Change notes, add notes, put melodies higher or lower.
Harmony—Change keys, add sharps and flats, change chord structures.
Form—Repeat parts, change the order of parts, add parts.
Rhythm—Change time signature, tempo, rhythm.
Tone color—Play parts of the theme with different instruments.

Canzona

A *canzona* is a composition written for instruments. It is written in the polyphonic form of the madrigal, but there are no sung voices. Brass instruments were becoming more developed and popular during the Renaissance. The sackbut, an early trombone; hunting horns; and early trumpet-like instruments were heard in the *canzona*.

Suite

Just as a suite of rooms in a hotel is a group of rooms, a suite of music is a group of compositions under one title. Suites originated as dances that were popular in the courts and palaces of the Renaissance. Each dance is called a movement, and those usually included were galliards and passepieds.

Palestrina (1526?–1594)

As a boy, Palestrina had a beautiful voice. He was sent to Rome to study and sing in the choir. Some of the leaders of the church wished to return to the simple chant, but Palestrina loved polyphony (music in parts). He decided to write a Mass using polyphony. There was constant harmony, and when one part stopped, another part began. People loved his "new music," and he was recognized as a great composer.

Josquin Des Prez (1445–1521)

Josquin Des Prez was one of the late composers of the Medieval period and an early composer of the Renaissance period. He was born in the Netherlands, but he spent most of his life in Italy. The "rebirth" of music centered in Italy around the Roman Catholic Church. Josquin Des Prez was commissioned to write music by many important people during his life. He mainly wrote for the church and composed many Masses and motets.

William Byrd (1540–1623)

William Byrd was a famous composer from England. He was the organist in Queen Elizabeth I's chapel as well as a composer. William Byrd and Thomas Tallis, another composer, were able to get a license to manufacture books, so that much of Byrd's music was printed. Byrd wrote many madrigals which are still performed today.

Thomas Morley (1557–1603)

During the Renaissance, England became an important musical center, and several famous composers emerged. Queen Elizabeth I encouraged religious and secular music. Madrigals were the favorite form of entertainment of the wealthy people, and Thomas Morley became a popular composer of the time. We are still able to enjoy his music today.

Giovanni Gabrieli (1557–1612)

Gabrieli was a late Renaissance composer from Italy, and his music shows many characteristics of the Baroque period. During the late Renaissance instruments became even more developed. Recorders were played in consorts, brass instruments were developed, and stringed instruments became more advanced. Gabrieli loved composing *canzonas*. He experimented with music in space, making use of the echoing choir lofts in the great cathedrals. His use of voices and instruments was innovative and paved the way to the Baroque period.

THE BAROQUE PERIOD (1600–1750)

The Baroque period marks a very fancy and ornamental time in the arts. Architecture and art contained an abundance of flowers, cupids, and fancy designs.

Music corresponded with frills, trills, and other ornaments. Literature and music displayed emotionalism and elaborate settings. The trends led to a new form of entertainment, *opera*. Instruments were developed even further, and instrumental music equaled vocal music in form and importance. Keyboard instruments included organ, clavichord, and harpsichord. Orchestras were created using high and low stringed instruments as well as more complicated woodwind and brass instruments. Music still was centered among the wealthy and the church.

Fugue

A *fugue* is a composition in which the theme is developed in counterpoint. Counterpoint is a form of polyphony which combines several melodic lines. It is much like a canon or round. In a canon the theme is repeated throughout, but in a fugue it is taken up and changed, with other melodic patterns weaving in and out. At times, the theme may not appear at all, and these sections are called *episodes*. It took a master of composition to control the melodic and harmonic lines of the fugue. The most accomplished composer of this art was J.S. Bach.

Prelude

A *prelude* is an instrumental work that is used as an introduction. Sometimes preludes were used as introductions to another piece of music or to a church service or other ceremony. A prelude is an independent instrumental composition that is improvised in nature and follows no special form. Preludes were most often performed on the organ.

Cantata

The *cantata* is a sacred or secular work for voices and instruments. It consists of a story or play that is sung by a chorus and soloists, but not acted. It contains arias and recitatives (speech songs) and is similar to an oratorio. The cantata is usually on a much smaller scale than an oratorio. They were often used during a church service to amplify the sermon. They used familiar hymn tunes called chorales.

Antonio Vivaldi (1675?–1741)

Vivaldi was not only a great composer, he was also a priest. The church was still the center of music, and the only other places a composer could be employed were in the castles and wealthy homes of noblemen. The music center of the world was now Venice, which was Vivaldi's home. Here he studied, taught, and wrote music. He is best known as the "Father of the Concerto." He was much admired by his contemporaries, and J.S. Bach transcribed several of his works for the harpsichord and organ.

Johann Sebastian Bach (1685–1750)

Johann Sebastian Bach was the greatest member of a well-known German musical family. He was a plain, hard-working man who never left Germany or traveled over 300 miles from home. He was orphaned as a young boy and was forced to live with a brother who did not want him. At fifteen he left his brother's home to attend choir school. Here he studied and became an accomplished musician and composer. Bach spent most of his adult life working in the church. After his first wife died he married again and had a total of twenty children. Bach composed preludes, toccatas, chorales, and all forms associated with the church. He was a genius in the art of the fugue. Some people believe he was the greatest composer who ever lived.

George Frederick Handel (1685–1759)

Handel and Bach were born in the same year, 1685. Bach was truly a Baroque composer and was the master of that era. Handel lived during the same time, but his music leans toward the Classical forms and styles. Handel began his career as a church organist in the cathedral, but he was attracted to the secular songs of the theater. He served as musician for the Hanover Court, but he eventually went to England where most of his works were composed. Perhaps his most famous work is the *Messiah*. He lived a successful life as a composer and musician until he became blind. But even then he continued to work in the field of music.

THE CLASSICAL PERIOD (1750–1815)

The Classical period finds musicians less dependent on the nobility and wealthy inhabitants of the castle. The church was still an important force along with the aristocracy, but now musicians could give lessons, hold public concerts, work on commission, and publish operas to earn a living. This took the music out of the clutches of the aristocracy and allowed the common people to also enjoy music. By this time, the orchestra was well defined, and a great deal of literature was written for its use. The piano had replaced the other keyboard instruments. Forms in music were established, and music took on a brilliant, refined, and elegant manner.

Opera

Opera, a form that was originated during the Baroque period, is a play that is sung. It was very popular during the Classical period, when opera houses were opened for the public. This enabled the common people to become familiar with the great music of the day, and it helped to bring music out of the hands of the aristocracy. Operas were elaborate with splendid costumes and scenery. They often dealt with the political and moral problems of the time. The dialogue of the opera used *recitative* (a part of the music that is sung in the rhythm and phrasing of ordinary speech). Major solos were called *arias*.

Sonata

The *sonata* is an instrumental form written for one, two, or three instruments. It was usually written for a keyboard instrument or for keyboard accompaniment featuring a solo instrument. Classical sonatas are divided into three major sections called movements. The most common arrangement is a long movement to set the character, a slower section, and then a short, fast movement with a finale.

Symphony

The word *symphony* dates back to Greek times and means "a sounding together." It is the most highly developed form of orchestral music, as it combines the voices of all instruments of the orchestra. Symphonies grew out of the Renaissance *canzona* and playing of consorts of instruments together. Gradually more instruments were added, and the form developed into a standard four-movement composition.

Wolfgang Amadeus Mozart (1756–1791)

Mozart was a "child wonder." He began music lessons at four, was composing at five, and was touring Europe and playing for royalty by the age of six. As he and his sister toured, their performances aroused great enthusiasm. This early success was reversed in later years. He married Constance Weber and, although they were devoted to each other, neither could manage their affairs and they were always in debt. Mozart achieved successes in opera, and he produced a vast amount of work in his short life. His last piece of music was a Requiem, or Mass for the dead, that was commissioned by a stranger. Mozart felt that he was writing it for himself, and he died before it was finished at the young age of thirty-five. He was buried in a lonely pauper's grave during a blizzard.

Franz Josef Haydn (1732–1809)

Haydn showed potential as a musician at an early age, and he began formal instruction at age six. He was often in trouble for not practicing and playing practical jokes. As a young boy he attended choir school, where he continued his studies in music. When his voice changed, he was dismissed. Much of his life was spent in the castles of the Esterhazy family. During his service, he wrote music of many kinds, including operas, symphonies, and string quartets.

THE ROMANTIC PERIOD (1815–1900)

The Romantic period was a time of emotionalism, nature, and fantasy. The music of this time left the strict structures of the Classical period and moved on to new forms. The supernatural was a favorite theme in art and literature as well as in music. Music was considered a force of expression rather than an elegant and conforming art as it had been during the Classical era.

String Quartet

The *string quartet* had its beginnings in the Renaissance with the development of consorts of stringed instruments. The standard string quartet uses two violins, one viola, and one cello. The string quartet is a very popular form of chamber music. Only four instruments are involved, but the four voices allow a variety of possibilities to the composer. This form was a very personal composition to the composer as well as to the performers and the audience.

Song Form

A song refers to a piece for one voice with or without instrumental accompaniment. Even Renaissance music used keyboard accompaniment with song forms.It was not until the Romantic period that an effort was made to bring the text and melody together in an intimate relationship. This was the goal of the Romantic song form.

Concerto

A concerto is a work in three or four movements in which one or more solo instruments are contrasted with a larger group of instruments. At first, the solo part was written for violin, but soon a variety of instruments were featured. Concertos were first written during the Baroque period, and they developed according to styles and practices popular during later eras.

Ludwig van Beethoven (1770–1827)

Beethoven is a bridge from the Classical to the Romantic periods of music. He learned from Mozart and Haydn, but he went on to the new ideas of the Romantic composers. He did not have a happy childhood and was forced to practice by his drunken father. He became a famed pianist and a favorite of the Viennese aristocracy. He composed slowly, working with sketches and fragments, changing and revising to perfect the finished product. He was known as a proud man, refusing to bow to royalty. He was also a man who loved nature, and he often composed on walks in the country with the sounds of nature around him. In his later years, he became deaf. This was a tragic loss for the composer, but it was not a defeat. Some of Beethoven's most beautiful music was composed after he became deaf.

Frédéric Chopin (1810–1849)

Chopin was a patriot with a deep love for his native Poland. Many of his compositions are based on Polish folk music. At the age of eight, he was an established pianist, and he published his first composition at the age of fifteen. He was a shy person who never married. Chopin was mainly a pianist and has been called "the poet of the piano." Although he was born in Poland and loved his country deeply, he spent most of his life in Paris, France.

Pyotr Ilyich Tchaikovsky (1840–1893)

Tchaikovsky was a Russian whose parents had little interest in music. He began piano lessons at age seven, but his studies led him to become a clerk in the

Ministry of Justice. Eventually he became disgusted with his life as a lawyer and decided to devote all his time to music. He became Professor of Harmony at the Moscow Conservatory. He was attracted to the theater and composed operas and ballets. Because of his innovative ideas, his works were sometimes not accepted. He was an extremely emotional person and was afflicted with epilepsy. He died of cholera in 1893.

THE TWENTIETH-CENTURY PERIOD (1900–   )

The twentieth century has seen tremendous technological and scientific development. Important advances are being made in manufacturing, transportation, and communication. Art and music also developed with new methods and styles through Expressionism and Impressionism, using electronics and dissonant harmonies. Composers left the formal rules of composition to experiment with chance music, twelve-tone music, and electronic music. The jazz medium also became popular and an accepted means of formal entertainment. This period is marked with experimentation and new forms and ideas that are still being explored today.

Chance Music

Chance music involves music put together by chance procedures, such as flipping a coin or rolling dice to choose rhythms, patterns, or chords. John Cage is a pioneer of this type of music, working with silence, sounds of nature, electronic sounds, and all sounds around us. There is no traditional continuity or coherence to the music, but a relationship of time and a neighboring relationship. Music of this type simply happens by chance, and it is up to the composer and audience to make sense of the random selections.

Electronic Music

For hundreds of years, the traditional instruments remained the same with the only new addition of the saxophone. With the development of electricity, however, a whole new family of instruments was introduced—the electronic instruments. One of the first was probably the electronic organ and amplification of certain instruments such as guitars. Today, the synthesizer is the ultimate electronic instrument. It can imitate almost any timbre of traditional instruments and create an infinity of additional sounds. At first, the synthesizer was not accepted as an "instrument" by serious composers, but today a good deal of modern music is written for the synthesizer.

Tone Row

Arnold Schoenberg was largely responsible for the development of the *tone row*. He was looking for new ways to use the chromatic tones of the tonal scale. The system he organized was a relationship of the twelve tones "only with one another." There was no tonic, and each tone was of equal importance. In each composition, a new arrangement of the twelve tones was used. Rules guiding the use of the tone row provided a theory in which each tone of the row must be used before repeating a tone. They could be used in various fashions of unison, combinations, retrograde, inversion, and transposition.

Jazz

Jazz arose at the beginning of the century in New Orleans. It was based upon a characteristic melodic line close to the spiritual song. Traditional harmonies were used with the addition of "blue" notes or "bended" notes. These, and its strong rhythmic beat and syncopation, form a combination that made jazz very popular by the turn of the century. The use of improvisation is also an element that makes jazz a unique form. At first, it was not accepted in certain circles of the music world, although composers used jazz elements in their works. Today, jazz is accepted as a form providing value and worth to the music world.

Béla Bartók (1881–1945)

Béla Bartók was born in a farming community in Hungary. From his earliest years, he was exposed to the peasant songs of his country. After his graduation from the academy in Budapest, he began a systematic study of these folk songs. He found that what many believed to be trivial songs of no great value were instead a treasure of works. Many were in old Greek modes or pentatonic scales with free and varied rhythms. Bartók incorporated these findings into his music to give it a nationalistic flavor.

Charles Ives (1874–1954)

Charles Ives was born in Danbury, Connecticut. He was taught by his father and later studied music at Yale University under Horatio Parker. At first, Ives made music his vocation, but he later entered business and composed in his spare time. His style was eclectic, and he combined many of the concepts of the twentieth century such as impressionistic devices, unusual rhythms, polytonality, dissonance, and experiments in sonority.

Igor Stravinsky (1882–1971)

Stravinsky was born in Russia in 1882. His father was a bass singer in the Imperial Opera, so he was raised in a musical family and studied music from an early age. He was a pupil of Rimsky-Korsakov, and his works soon gained success. His first ballet was *The Firebird,* and from there he went on to compose many other fine ballets. He employed new ideas of bitonality, polytonality, and rhythmic innovations. These concepts made his works very controversial. The first time *Rite of Spring* was performed, it caused a riot! He was a man of the future who helped transport music from the old ideas of the Romantic period to the new ideas of the twentieth century.

October

"Movin' and Groovin' "

"What's Brewing in Music?"

MOVIN' AND GROOVIN': The Bulletin Board

Objective: Students will improve their motor skills through movement, routines, and dances.

Materials Needed:

Dark blue background paper
Yellow construction paper
White construction paper
Black felt-tip pen
Scissors
Straight pins

Construction Directions:

1. Use an overhead projector or transparency to trace the letters onto the yellow construction paper. Cut out the letters and attach to the background paper with straight pins.

2. Trace the skeletons onto white construction paper. Draw the features and bones with a black felt-tip pen. Cut out the skeletons and attach them to the background with straight pins. Pin the arms and legs to the bones. Then fold out slightly to give a three-dimensional effect. (NOTE: You might want to use commercially prepared paper skeletons instead.)

MOVIN' AND GROOVIN': Unit Activities

Movement to music improves students' basic motor skills and is an activity that they all enjoy. It can be used as an interpretive experience, a mechanical extension of music, or as an activity to capture the interest of the class. As movement activities progress some teachers may want to avoid the word "dance" and substitute words such as "positions," "movements," or "routines." The series of lessons in this unit will start with some basic movements, including walking, skipping, sliding, and running. They will advance to simple dances and movement games such as circle dances and simple routines. Final lessons will involve square-dance steps and creating an entire routine to a specific song. Students need to be aware of weight distribution, balance, and body position as they study movement. Arrange the skeletons on the board in various positions each day and have students "copy" these positions. Let a student arrange a skeleton for the class to imitate. They may discover that certain positions are impossible to maintain because of weight and balance.

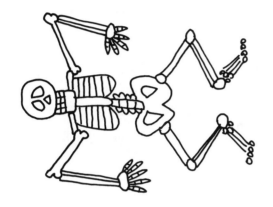
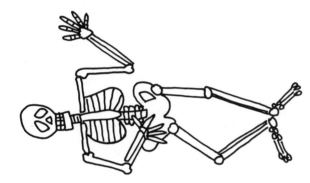
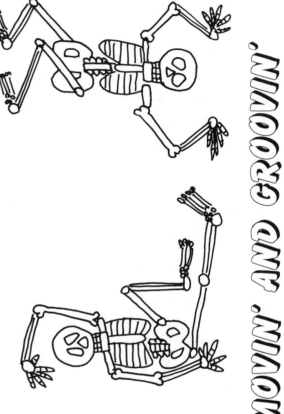
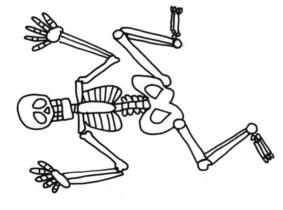
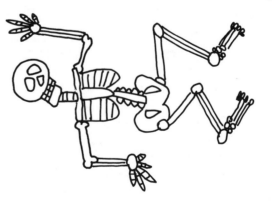

MOVIN' AND GROOVIN'

SIMPLE MOVEMENT SONGS

The following four songs teach the basic motor skills of walking, skipping, sliding, and running. Students should learn to sing the songs and then try to use the appropriate movements as they sing. Song words stress staying with the beat as well as performing the proper movement.

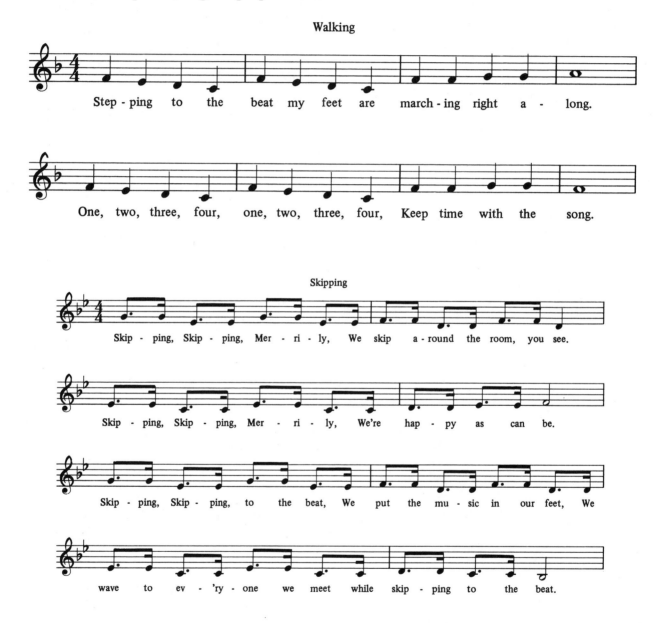

Walking

Step - ping to the beat my feet are march - ing right a - long.

One, two, three, four, one, two, three, four, Keep time with the song.

Skipping

Skip - ping, Skip - ping, Mer - ri - ly, We skip a - round the room, you see.

Skip - ping, Skip - ping, Mer - ri - ly, We're hap - py as can be.

Skip - ping, Skip - ping, to the beat, We put the mu - sic in our feet, We

wave to ev - 'ry - one we meet while skip - ping to the beat.

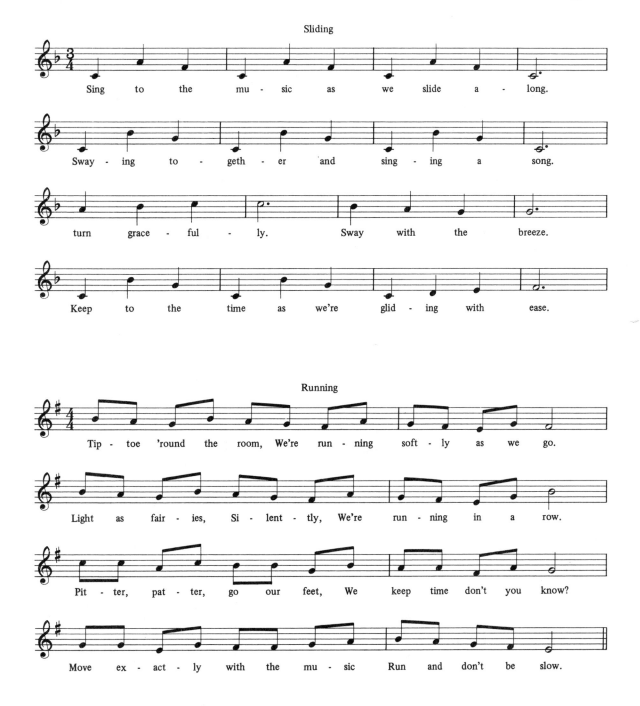

MOVE TO THE MUSIC

Students should have many experiences which involve movement to music. After students have learned the four songs which identify various types of movements, the teacher should play examples and see if students can move correctly. This is a testing device for the teacher, but it is a game for the students. Examples are to be mixed, and in between each one the students must stand still "like statues." The teacher may use the following examples, use song material in this book, or make up appropriate music.

LISTEN AND MOVE

Rhythms played on the piano are usually well defined. It becomes more difficult to listen to a recorded composition with orchestra and choose the correct movement. The teacher should choose recorded examples that demonstrate walking, skipping, sliding, running, and tiptoe rhythms. Choose examples that are very clear such as:

Walking— "Jesu, Joy of Man's Desiring" (Bach)
           Aria from "The Water Music Suite" (Handel)
           "March of the Siamese Children" from *King and I* (Rogers)

Sliding— "Tales From the Vienna Woods" (Strauss)
         "Waltz of the Flowers" from *Nutcracker Suite* (Tchaikovsky)
         "Music Box Waltz" from *Ballet Suite No. 1* (Shostakovich)

Tiptoe—   "Dance of the Sugar Plum Fairy" from *Nutcracker Suite* (Tchaikovsky)
             "Dance of the Flutes" from *Nutcracker Suite* (Tchaikovsky)
             "March" from *Memories of Childhood* (Pinto)
Running—   "Country Dance" (Beethoven)
             "Flight of the Bumble Bee" (Rimsky-Korsakov)
             "Run Run" from *Memories of Childhood* (Pinto)
Skipping—   "Theme and Variation on Pop Goes the Weasel" (Calliet)
             Fourth movement of *Second Piano Concerto* (Brahms)
             "Over the Hills" (Grainger)

This activity may extend to interpretive movement. Before beginning the activity students should discuss different types of music and how music makes them feel. Sad, slow music would not have the same movement as happy, fast music. Play different types of music and allow students to "act it out." They may respond to the activity better if they have something in their hands such as scarves, balloons, or streamers. This would be a good place to introduce ballet to the class through simple movements, books, filmstrips, or videos.

DRUM TALK

A further extension of the movement concept is demonstrated as students play rhythms on the drums. Have each student come forward and ask him or her to play one of the rhythms. These may be notated on the board as follows:

After students have mastered the ability to play these rhythms on the drum, the teacher can extend the game once again. Choose a student to come to the drum. This student chooses one of the rhythms, but he or she doesn't tell the class. As the student plays the rhythm the class should move correctly to the rhythm. When the drum stops students become still "like statues."

TIMBRE TALK

Because concepts need to be reinforced many times, students may become bored with the same games. "Timbre Talk" is a variation of "Drum Talk." The teacher should be behind the piano or in back of the room, out of the sight of the students. Various rhythms are played (walking, running, skipping, sliding, etc.) on a variety of instruments. Students must identify the instrument and the movement. Next, have five groups, each assigned to a different instrument (example: Group 1, woodblock; 2, drum; 3, triangle; 4, cymbals; 5, xylophone). Each group may move only when its instrument plays. The teacher plays various rhythms on the instruments and the correct group must respond with the correct movement. Be careful not to always play the same rhythm on the same instrument or students will associate one timbre with one movement.

FOLLOW ALONG

Students are in a circle for this game, with one student in the center of the circle. The teacher must choose a record that has a steady beat and that is not too fast or too slow. In upper grades pop music could be used. The student in the center does different movements to the beat in sets of eight (eight claps, eight bends, eight sways, etc.). The class must follow the movement and keep in time with the beat. At first the person in the center may have difficulty thinking what to do. Give the class many suggestions before they begin. As they repeat the activity ideas will come more readily. Students in upper grades should be encouraged to use more sophisticated steps and movements.

CIRCLE GAMES

Many circle games such as "Farmer in the Dell," "Ring Around the Roses," "Hokey Pokey," "Looby Loo," etc. are traditional for students. In addition to these the teacher may use a creative lesson to accommodate a movement activity. This lesson should first be done as a class effort to give the students guidance. Choose a familiar song and make up new words that indicate movement. The following two songs are examples:

(To the tune of "Twinkle, Twinkle")

Step slide, step slide to the right,
Step slide to the left so light.
Turn around and touch your toe,
Clap your hands and don't be slow,
Step slide, step slide to the right,
Step slide to the left so light.

(To the tune of "Yankee Doodle")

Marching, marching 'round the circle,
Turn and march the other way,
Marching forward, marching backward,
At attention stay!

Give a class assignment to upper-grade students to write this type of song on their own. The teacher may choose the best two examples for the class to perform.

STORY MOVEMENT

Story movement could begin with a discussion of animals and descriptions of how they move (for example, lions, birds, elephants, and rabbits). Next, read the story, "Wilbur the Lion" and let the class talk about what movements the animals would make. As the teacher tells the story, students should make the appropriate movements.

Wilbur the Lion

Wilbur the lion prowled through the jungle. He stretched and yawned, and then he roared, "I am the King of the Jungle." On he went, with his head held high, daring anyone to come near. Wilbur looked into the distance where he could see monkeys in the trees. They were swinging from branch to branch and having such a good time. Wilbur decided that he would join in the fun. He raced toward the trees roaring, "Here comes the King! I am the King!"

All the monkeys began squealing and chattering as they swung away through the trees. Wilbur sat down sadly. It was lonely being King of the Jungle. Everyone was afraid of him.

He leaned back against the tree and a tear slid down his face. Over by the river he could see elephants swinging their trunks and spraying each other with water. It looked so refreshing, but he knew better than to try to join in. Yesterday he had almost been trampled by a huge mother elephant when he tried to play with her baby.

He remembered the zebras last week. They galloped around playing hide and seek. Wilbur had played too and jumped out suddenly with a roar. The zebras didn't think it was funny! He had to run for his life or be stampeded by the entire herd.

Just then Wilbur heard a "tweet-tweet" and looked up to see a baby bird jumping from a limb. The baby tried bravely to fly for the very first time and he did soar for a moment. Then he came crashing to the ground. The mother and father birds flew wildly about. They pecked Wilbur on the head and pulled on his tail. But Wilbur picked up the baby bird in his mouth and began climbing up the tree. Gently he put the little bird back in the nest, where he snuggled in with his brothers and sisters.

The mother and father birds were so happy they flew all over the jungle chirping and telling how Wilbur had saved their baby. From then on the other animals were not afraid when Wilbur went prowling and roaring through the jungle. He joined in all the games and had many friends ever after.

After interpreting this story with movement, the whole class or individuals could make up other stories that suggest movement. Some titles might be "The Circus," "Transportation," "The Farm," "Outer Space," and "The Haunted Graveyard."

ROUTINES

Upper grades may continue movement in the form of routines. Students will be familiar with routines if there is a cheering section in the high school that performs routines at half-time. Other students have watched music videos, other cheerleaders, or dance performances. Begin simple routines with a series of eight or sixteen counts for each action. Students will enjoy working with current pop music that has a strong beat. As students advance make movements more intricate. It is possible to divide the class up in groups and have each group create a routine to the same song. Stress precision of movement and staying together as the routine is performed. A simple routine might be as follows:

Simple Eight-Count Routine

(In a line facing front) Clap and bend knees to the beat.

(Turn in a line, everyone facing right) Clap hands and bend knees.

(In a line facing back) Clap hands and bend knees.

(Turn in a line, everyone facing left) Clap hands and bend knees.

(Everyone facing front) Put hands in the air. Gradually lower arms until everyone has their arms on the shoulders of the person on each side of him. Take the full eight beats to do this.

(Everyone facing front with hands still on shoulders) Raise knees in high marching steps in place for eight counts.

(Everyone facing front with hands still on shoulders) March four steps forward and four steps back.

(Everyone turn to the right. Put hands on shoulders of person in front) March in place eight steps.

(Everyone turn facing to the back. Hands on shoulders of person on each side) March in place eight counts.

(Same position to the back) March four counts forward and four counts back.

(Everyone turn to the left. Put hands on shoulders of the person in front) March in place eight steps.

(Everyone turn to the front. Hands on own waist) March in place eight steps.

(Everyone do "twist" movement at hips) Gradually bend knees lowering to eight counts

(Face front and do "twist" movement at hips) Gradually raising to eight counts.

Repeat routine until end of record. Last movement everyone drops to right knee with hands stretched high in the air.

OUTSIDE RESOURCES

There are many outside resources to call upon for help with movement in upper grades. A high school or junior high cheerleader could teach the students steps and claps to cheers. The teacher would need to approve cheers to be done because some might have too much movement for the classroom. The band major or majorette might take students outside and teach them the rudiments of marching. This is a movement that requires precision in time and formation. Local dance instructors can be called upon to show the different movements of jazz, ballet, and modern dance. Students can be encouraged to try basic steps. If dance instructors are not available, perhaps an advanced student in dancing could provide instruction. Square dance clubs may have members who will demonstrate and teach basic concepts of square dancing. If a college is near, there may be a wealth of foreign students who are willing to perform dances of their countries. The possibilities of outside resources are unlimited if the teacher is willing to seek them.

SQUARE DANCE

When beginning to teach the basic steps of square dancing the teacher should walk through steps until they have been mastered. Even first grade students can learn basic steps, but such steps are appropriate for any age. Many adult square dance classes begin with the same basic steps. After students can walk through the steps try to do the dance with the music.

Circle Left

All students hold hands in a large circle and move to the left.

Circle Right

All students hold hands in a large circle and move to the right.

Bow to Your Partner

Partners face each other. Boys bow and girls curtsy.

Swing Your Partner

Partners link right elbows and walk around each other.

Do-Si-Do

Partners stand back-to-back. They walk around each other (pass backs then pass fronts).

Girls to the Center

Girls step to the center while boys stay outside circle. Girls join right hands in center and walk forward.

Boys to the Center

Boys step to the center while girls stay outside circle. Boys join right hands in center and walk forward.

Promenade

Partners stand side-by-side. Boy crosses his wrists and girl holds his hands without crossing hers. They walk side-by-side with boy on right side of girl around circle. Alternate version: Partners stand side-by-side with boy on right side of girl. Boy has left arm over girl's shoulder and she holds his left hand at her shoulder with her left hand. Boy is holding girl's right hand with his right hand at his waist. They walk side-by-side around the circle.

WHAT'S BREWING IN MUSIC?: The Bulletin Board

Objective: Students will improve their knowledge of music symbols with flash cards, worksheets, and their music textbooks.

Materials Needed:

White background paper
Construction paper (black, light green, brown)
Black yarn
Tissue paper (light blue, yellow, orange)
Scissors
Straight pins
Glue
Black felt-tip pen

WHAT'S BREWING IN MUSIC ?

Construction Directions:

1. Use an opaque projector or transparencies to make the letters on the background.
2. Trace the kettle, witch's robe, and hat onto black construction paper.
3. Trace the witch's face and hands onto light green construction paper using a black felt-tip pen.
4. Trace the logs and spoon out of brown construction paper. A real wooden spoon would be very effective if available.
5. Cut out and attach the witch and kettle to the board with straight pins. Pull the paper slightly away for a three-dimensional effect.
6. Pin on the spoon and logs.
7. Use red and orange tissue paper to cut out as flames. Pin these flames just at the bottom so that the flames will go up around the kettle.
8. Pin crinkled blue tissue paper inside the kettle for a bubbling effect.
9. Pin black yarn to the board for steam and the witch's hair.
10. Use black construction paper for the music symbols and pin them to the steam. (NOTE: You might want to just mark the symbols directly onto the background paper with a black felt-tip pen.)

WHAT'S BREWING IN MUSIC?: Unit Activities

What's brewing in music? It could be anything that the class is studying during October. Whatever the subject, the teacher should have examples of that boiling in the smoke coming out of the witch's pot. This bulletin board displays music symbols. Ten activity pages follow, beginning with very simple color pages and progressing to harder worksheets. The teacher can use these as masters and copy additional sheets, games, or puzzles for the class. These activities may be simplified for the lower grades or advanced for students in upper grades. The teacher may put up the witch and pot first and then let students add symbols as they are presented and discussed in each class. When a new song is presented all symbols may be removed from the board. Let students put up only the symbols that are used in that particular song. Each day and class the symbols will change depending on the song material being used.

COLOR PUZZLE

Make copies of the "Color Puzzle" activity sheet and distribute them to students. The purpose of the puzzle is to make young students aware of various music symbols. You may change the symbols to fit any area your students are studying.

HALLOWEEN SYMBOL COLOR PAGE

Make copies of the "Halloween Symbol Color Page" and distribute them to students. This sheet helps students recognize music symbols. After students have colored the figures, you should point out these symbols in music books.

SYMBOL FLASH CARDS

One of the fastest methods of learning is drill. The teacher should make flash cards with music symbols on them. They can be made of a quarter sheet of construction paper, $5'' \times 7''$ cards, or any other durable, stiff paper. As the teacher holds them in front of the class, students say the name of the symbol together. After students are able to do this successfully, the teacher may want to make four sets of flash cards. Students are divided into four groups and a leader is chosen to show cards in each group. Students take turns answering and if the answer is correct the student gets the card. If a student cannot answer correctly the leader goes to the next student. The student with the most cards at the end of the game is the winner.

MIXED-UP SYMBOLS

Copy the "Mixed-Up" words onto a worksheet and draw in a blank. Students must write the correct word in the blank. The answers are given in the examples below.

1. E F I N _(Fine)_
2. F T A S F _(Staff)_
3. R E E A P T _(Repeat)_
4. L T F A _(Flat)_
5. A H R S P _(Sharp)_
6. F L E C _(Clef)_
7. I R B D S   Y E E _(Bird's eye)_
8. A U R N A T L _(Natural)_
9. C E A N C T _(Accent)_
10. Y I N D M C A S _(Dynamics)_
11. I T E M   N I S A R G T U E _(Time signature)_
12. T C A S O C A T _(Staccato)_
13. E S M R E A U _(Measure)_
14. A B R   I N L E _(Bar Line)_

15. F R T O E _____(Forte)_____
16. K Y E   T U G R A S I N E _____(Key signature)_____
17. O U L D E B   A B R _____(Double bar)_____
18. I A O P N _____(Piano)_____
19. I E T _____(Tie)_____
20. R U S L _____(Slur)_____

SYMBOL WORD PUZZLE

Make copies of the "Symbol Word Puzzle" and distribute them to students. This crossword puzzle reinforces students' knowledge of music symbol words, such as staff, clef, and space.

TIME SIGNATURE

Make copies of the "Time Signature" worksheet and distribute them to students. This sheet gives students practice in figuring out the counts in each measure and writing correct time signatures.

TREASURE HUNT

Make copies of the "Treasure Hunt" worksheet and distribute them to students. Students are to look in their music textbook for examples of particular symbols and write the page numbers on the worksheet.

MATCHING SYMBOLS

Make copies of the "Matching Symbols" worksheet and distribute them to students. Students are to match words to the correct symbols.

SYMBOL BLANKS

Make copies of the "Symbol Blanks" activity sheet and then distribute to students. Students are to fill in the blanks with the correct music symbols.

SYMBOL BOOK QUESTIONS

Before making copies of the "Symbol Book Questions" worksheet, you must find specific pages in the regular music text that has the examples shown on the worksheet. Fill in each page number before making copies of the worksheet. Students are to look up the page and fill in the blank with the correct answer.

Name_____ **Date**_____

COLOR PUZZLE

Use the color key at the bottom of this sheet to fill in the picture. When finished, what do you see?

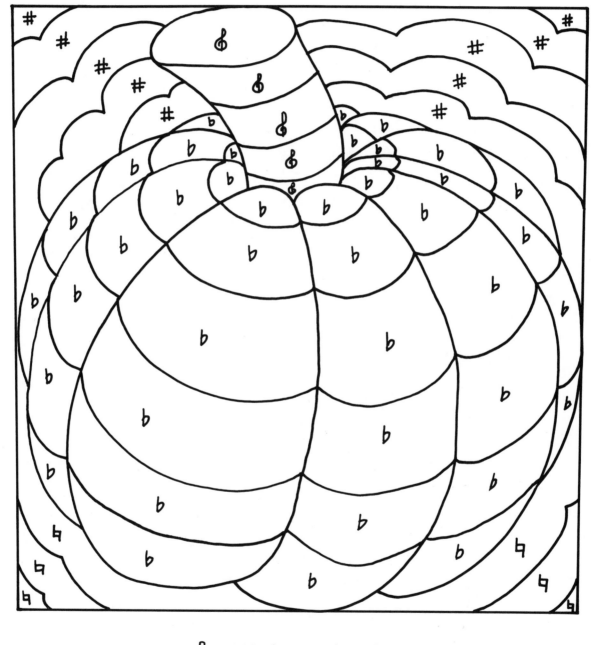

 = GREEN   # = YELLOW

♭ = ORANGE   ♮ = BLUE

HALLOWEEN SYMBOL COLOR PAGE

Use the color key at the bottom of this sheet to fill in these pictures.

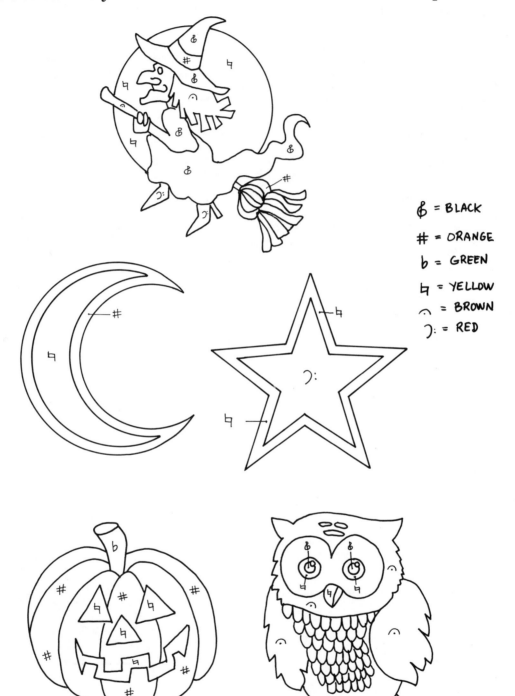

𝄻 = BLACK

♯ = ORANGE

♭ = GREEN

♮ = YELLOW

⌢ = BROWN

𝄢 = RED

Name _____ **Date** _____

TIME SIGNATURE

    Part One: Tell how many counts are in each measure and what kind of note gets one count for each of the following time signatures:

a. 4 _____   c. 6 _____   e. 3 _____

     4 _____   8 _____   2 _____

b. 12 _____   d. C _____   f. ₵ _____

     8 _____   _____   _____

    Part Two: Fill in each measure with the correct number of counts according to the time signature:

a. $\frac{4}{4}$ | | | | ‖

b. $\frac{6}{8}$ | | | | ‖

c. ₵ | | | | ‖

    Part Three: Write the correct time signature on the line in front of each measure:

SYMBOL WORD PUZZLE

Read the clues at the bottom of this sheet and fill in the crossword puzzle.

ACROSS
2. Name for short, choppy notes
4. Bass _____
5. Lowers a note one half-step
9. Medium
10. This is in a staff
11. Raises a note one half-step

DOWN
1. This has five lines and four spaces
3. The extra section at the end of a song
6. This is in a staff
7. _____ signature
8. To do over again

TREASURE HUNT

Look in your music textbook to find each of the following examples. When you have found the example, write the page number on the line. You might find many pages for one example, so write only one or two page numbers.

Find the Page . . .

_____ 1. With a treble clef

_____ 2. With a bass clef

_____ 3. That has *D.C. al fine*

_____ 4. With a 𝄐

_____ 5. With the repeat sign :‖

_____ 6. With $\frac{6}{8}$ time signature

_____ 7. With $\frac{4}{4}$ time signature

_____ 8. With $\frac{2}{4}$ time signature

_____ 9. With a C chord

_____ 10. With a natural sign

_____ 11. With two flats in the key signature

_____ 12. With a very loud dynamic marking, *ff*

_____ 13. With six staves in the song

_____ 14. With a soft dynamic marking, *p*

_____ 15. With staccato notes

_____ 16. With accents

_____ 17. Where the time signature changes during the song

_____ 18. With four measures in the first staff

_____ 19. With "cut time" ₵

_____ 20. With ten staves in the song

MATCHING SYMBOLS

Draw a line from each word on the left to the proper symbol on the right.

1.	Flat	a.	▤
2.	Sharp	b.	*ff*
3.	Slur	c.	‖
4.	Tie	d.	$^6_8$
5.	Phrase	e.	♮
6.	Bass clef	f.	▤
7.	Accent	g.	▷
8.	Very loud	h.	:‖
9.	Cut time	i.	*f*
10.	Bird's eye	j.	♪♪♪♪ ♪♪♪♪
11.	Double bar	k.	*mf*
12.	Measure	l.	>
13.	Treble clef	m.	𝄞##
14.	Medium loud	n.	C
15.	Time signature	o.	𝄐
16.	Staff	p.	◁
17.	Staccato	q.	▤
18.	Repeat	r.	𝄢
19.	Crescendo	s.	*pp*
20.	Key signature	t.	....
21.	Natural	u.	♯
22.	Very soft	v.	𝄞
23.	Common time	w.	▤
24.	Decrescendo	x.	¢
25.	Forte	y.	♭

SYMBOL BLANKS

Fill in each blank with the correct music symbol.

_____ 1. Draw the bass clef

_____ 2. This means to raise a note one half-step

_____ 3. The symbol for very loud

_____ 4. This tells us to hold a note longer

_____ 5. This means to lower the note one half-step

_____ 6. Draw a treble clef

_____ 7. This has five lines and four spaces

_____ 8. This symbol tells us to repeat

_____ 9. Repeat until *Fine*

_____ 10. Time signature with four counts to a measure, and a quarter note gets one count

_____ 11. The symbol for very soft

_____ 12. The symbol that cancels a sharp or flat

_____ 13. Time signature with six counts to a measure, and the eighth note gets one count

_____ 14. Sign to gradually get louder

_____ 15. Sign to gradually get softer

_____ 16. Symbol for staccato notes

_____ 17. Letters that stand for medium loud

_____ 18. Sign for "end of song"

_____ 19. Symbol that stands for "cut time"

_____ 20. Symbol to show a note is accented

SYMBOL BOOK QUESTIONS

Look at each page number filled in below by your teacher. You are to look up the page in your regular music text and fill in the blank with the correct answer.

1. On page _____, what is the time signature? _____

2. On page _____, there are _____ counts in the measure.

3. On page _____, what kind of note gets one count? _____

4. On page _____, what word is the *fermata* above? _____

5. On page _____, what staff is the word *Fine* above? _____

6. On page _____, how many staves are in the song? _____

7. On page _____, what are the three chords above the staves? _____, _____, _____

8. On page _____, what is the dynamic level of the song? _____

9. On page _____, how many sharps are in the key signature? _____

10. On page _____, which staff do you repeat to? _____

11. On page _____, how many flats are in the key signature? _____

12. On page _____, the time signature changes. What does it start at? _____ What does it change to? _____

13. On page _____, how many natural signs are on staff two? _____

14. On page _____, which staff has staccato notes? _____

15. On page _____, there are how many counts in each measure? _____

16. On page _____, how many measures are in the song? _____

17. On page _____, how many accented notes are in the song? _____

18. On page _____, which staff has a crescendo marking? _____

19. On page _____, which staff has a ritard marking? _____

20. On page _____, how many ties are in the song? _____

OCTOBER ANSWER KEY

Color Puzzle

A pumpkin will be seen.

Time Signature

Part One:

    a. 4/quarter
    b. 12/eighth
    c. 6/eighth
    d. 4/quarter
    e. 3/half
    f. 2/half

Part Two: Answers will vary.

Part Three:

    a. $\frac{3}{4}$
    b. $\frac{6}{8}$
    c. $\frac{3}{2}$

Symbol Word Puzzle

Across:	Down:
2. Staccato	1. Staff
4. Clef	3. Coda
5. Flat	6. Line
9. Mezzo	7. Time
10. Space	8. Repeat
11. Sharp	

Treasure Hunt

Answers will vary.

Matching Symbols

1.	y	10.	o	18.	h
2.	u	11.	c	19.	p
3.	f	12.	a	20.	m
4.	w	13.	v	21.	e
5.	j	14.	k	22.	s
6.	r	15.	d	23.	n
7.	l	16.	q	24.	g
8.	b	17.	t	25.	i
9.	x				

Symbol Blanks

1. 𝄢

2. ♯

3. ff

4. 𝄐

5. ♭

6. 𝄞

7. (staff lines)

8. 𝄇

9. D.C. al fine

10. 4/4

11. *pp*

12. ♮

13. 6/8

14. (crescendo)

15. (decrescendo)

16. ..

17. *mf*

18. ‖

19. ₵

20. <

Symbol Book Questions

Answers will vary.

November

"Missing Mystery Instrument"

"Turkey Tunes"

MISSING MYSTERY INSTRUMENT: The Bulletin Board

Objective: Students will increase their knowledge of musical instruments by listening, playing, and doing written work about instruments.

Materials Needed:

Light yellow background paper
Construction paper (black, white)
Felt-tip pens in various colors
Scissors
Straight pins

Construction Directions:

1. Use an opaque projector or transparency to trace the lettering onto the black construction paper. Attach the cut-out letters to the background with straight pins.

2. Trace the figures onto white construction paper and color as desired with felt-tip markers.

3. Cut out the figures and attach them to the background paper with straight pins. Pull the figures away from the board to give a three-dimensional effect.

4. Make notes out of black construction paper and attach around the figures if desired.

MISSING MYSTERY INSTRUMENT: Unit Activities

This bulletin board is an introduction to a unit on instruments. It will catch students' interest as they come into the room guessing what each musician is playing. Look at each position and determine which instrument is being played. If possible have pictures of the instruments. In early grades the teacher may want to limit the study to instruments found in the classroom and a few instruments of the orchestra. Each year, using the worksheets, games, puzzles, and suggestions provided, students should increase their knowledge of this subject. The teacher may wish to feature one instrument each class period. Only that "Missing Mystery Instrument" would be on the board. Students should have pictures of the instruments to choose from and which they can put on the bulletin board in the right position. Each day a new instrument could be added until all instruments have been studied and the bulletin board is complete.

INSTRUMENTS AROUND THE ROOM

Early studies of instruments should emphasize those found in the classroom. Students should learn to identify them both by sight and sound. The teacher may choose to introduce a new instrument each week to beginning students. They

MISSING MYSTERY INSTRUMENT

should look at it, hear it, and play it. Review instruments each week until students can play each instrument in the room and identify it by sight and by sound. The teacher can make a game of it by standing in the back of the room, behind the students, and playing each instrument. Students must identify the instrument by its sound without looking.

INTRODUCING INSTRUMENTS OF THE ORCHESTRA

An excellent teaching tool for the introduction of instruments of the orchestra is *Peter and the Wolf*. There are many versions including films, videos, and records available. Young students love the story, and the instruments used are easily recognized because of the characters they represent. After *Peter and the Wolf* use other recordings with the same instruments until students can identify them easily in all recordings. Gradually introduce more instruments until all instruments of the orchestra can be identified by sight and sound and categorized in families. The Bomar filmstrips and posters are an excellent teaching aid. There are other posters and filmstrips available, or the teacher may make a set by cutting pictures from magazines and pasting them on posters. The worksheets, games, and puzzles in this chapter provide stimulating activities for the study of musical instruments.

I'M GOING ON A TRIP

This game may begin with young students learning instruments in the classroom. The first student says, "I'm going on a trip and I'm going to take a *drum*." The next student says "I'm going on a trip and I'm going to take a drum and some *bells*." Each student must add something to the list. If he or she cannot remember previous instruments, he or she is out. Older students can play the game by using all the instruments of the orchestra.

SOUND COMPOSITION

Using percussion instruments found in the classroom, students can compose a sound composition. As a class project discuss a topic, such as "The Haunted House." Talk about things found in a haunted house, noises heard, and instruments that could be used for those sounds. Next, list events in sequence to construct the sound composition and which instruments will be used:

1. Walking up to house—woodblock
2. Squeaking door opening—sandblock
3. Walking into house—woodblock
4. Door slamming shut—bass drum
5. Skeletons rattling—xylophone
6. Pounding on door to get out—bongo drums
7. Running to another door—woodblock

8. Chains rattling—tambourine
9. Ghosts flying by—maraca
10. Skeletons and ghosts chasing upstairs—woodblock, xylophone, maraca
11. Running in room and slamming door shut—woodblock, bass drum
12. Moaning—triangle
13. All goblins chasing down stairs—woodblock, tambourine, xylophone, maraca, triangle
14. Pounding on door to get out—bass drum
15. Door opens and running away—woodblock (fading)

Practice each of the fifteen steps, then play the composition. Record the final results and let students evaluate their sound composition. Other titles that might be chosen include "The Thunder Storm," "Jungle Life," "Traffic Sounds," "Playground Sounds," and "Walk in the Woods."

INSTRUMENT BINGO

Bingo cards may be made by following the sample card below.

Strings	Woodwind	Brass	Percussion
Guitar	Clarinet	Tuba	Triangle
Violin	Saxophone	Trumpet	Gong
Mandolin	Oboe	Baritone	Bell
Cello	Flute	French Horn	Maraca

"Bingos" may only count across, because there are limited instruments in each family and it is too easy to get a "Bingo" vertically. The teacher should make the cards and mix up the instruments to make as many combinations as possible. No two cards can be identical. The teacher calls instruments under families, such as "under the brass family, a French horn," or "under the string family, a mandolin." The first person who "Bingos" is the winner. Instruments that might be included on cards are as follows:

STRINGS	*WOODWIND*	*BRASS*	*PERCUSSION*
Violin	Flute	Tuba	Triangle
Viola	Piccolo	French horn	Bells
Lute	Clarinet	Trumpet	Xylophone
Cello	Bass clarinet	Cornet	Castanet
Bass viol	Oboe	Bugle	Bass drum
Harp	Saxophone	Baritone	Snare drum
Guitar	English horn	Trombone	Kettle drum
Mandolin	Bassoon		Bongo drum
Banjo	Contrabassoon		Gong
			Maraca
			Marimba
			Piano
			Clavichord
			Harpsichord

FAMILY STAND

Divide the class into four groups with the following family names: Strings, Woodwinds, Brass, and Percussion. Play any recording of instrumental music. When an instrument or family of instruments is playing that group should stand up. At times more than one group will be standing, and all groups will be standing if all families of instruments are being played together. At first use recordings where only one instrument or family is heard. The examples should be short and when the correct family is standing move to the next recording. This activity is appropriate for both beginning and advanced students. The examples selected should suit their ages and capabilities.

INSTRUMENT FLASH CARDS

Flash cards may be made by using coloring books, song books, or magazines that contain pictures of instruments. Copy the pictures and paste them on five-by-seven cards. Have the family and name of instrument on back of each card. Students may show them to each other and name both the family and the instrument. The winner of the game is the person or group who can name the most instruments.

BAND DEMONSTRATION

During the course of the study of musical instruments have high-school students come in and demonstrate various instruments. Younger students will be thrilled to see and hear the instruments "live," and older students are delighted to perform. Even older students enjoy hearing their own classmates perform. This could be extended to a classroom trip to a band or orchestra rehearsal or concert. Encourage students to write about their trip and their thoughts and feelings about the rehearsal or concert.

MIXED-UP INSTRUMENTS

Copy the "Mixed-Up" words onto a work sheet and leave blanks. Students must write the correct word in the blank. The answers are given for the examples below.

1. N L I V O I _____(Violin)_____
2. T L U F E _____(Flute)_____
3. T T R P M U E _____(Trumpet)_____
4. R U D M _____(Drum)_____
5. I O L A V _____(Viola)_____
6. C I C P L O O _____(Piccolo)_____
7. N O H R _____(Horn)_____
8. L R I N T A G E _____(Triangle)_____
9. L E C O L _____(Cello)_____
10. C R E T I L A N _____(Clarinet)_____
11. Y L H N P E O X O _____(Xylophone)_____
12. R G O N A _____(Organ)_____
13. U T A G I R _____(Guitar)_____
14. E R S T E Z Y H I N S _____(Synthesizer)_____
15. T R B U I O N M A E _____(Tambourine)_____
16. R M O T N B O E _____(Trombone)_____
17. S L E B L _____(Bells)_____
18. S A B S _____(Bass)_____
19. X A O H S N E P O _____(Saxophone)_____
20. U B T A _____(Tuba)_____
21. Y B C A L M _____(Cymbal)_____
22. P A O I N _____(Piano)_____
23. B O O E _____(Oboe)_____
24. A S O O S B N _____(Bassoon)_____
25. P H A R _____(Harp)_____

26. N A O B J (Banjo)
27. C W L O D B O O K (Woodblock)
28. T A S A N C T E (Castanet)
29. M R C A A A (Maraca)
30. N G G O (Gong)

INSTRUMENT WORDSEARCH

Make copies of the "Instrument Wordsearch" and distribute to students for them to solve.

INSTRUMENT FAMILY PUZZLE

Make copies of the "Instrument Family Puzzle" and distribute them to students. This activity sheet helps reinforce knowledge of brass, string, percussion, and woodwind instruments.

INSTRUMENT CROSSWORD PUZZLE

Make copies of the "Instrument Crossword Puzzle" and distribute them to students. This puzzle reinforces students' knowledge of such instruments as the bassoon, piccolo, and oboe.

INSTRUMENT RIDDLES

Make copies of the "Instrument Riddles" worksheet and distribute them to students. Students are to answer each riddle with the name of an instrument.

Name _____ Date _____

INSTRUMENT WORDSEARCH

Look at the instrument names at the bottom of this sheet and find each one in the wordsearch below. The words can be found either horizontally or vertically.

```
A V I O L A R C E L L O T S P
B I C E I G E H D G F B A S S
J O K L M U C P I A N O N O P
F L U T E I O I Q R S E T F C
U I V R W T R C X G Y Z W R Y
A N T U B A D C E O X C O E M
B C D M A R E O F N Y L O N B
H A R P S G R L H G L A D C A
I J K E S L B O N G O R B H L
M N O T O R G A N B P I L H B
P Q T R O M B O N E H N O O A
T R I A N G L E R L O E C R N
C A S T A N E T S L N T K N J
T S A X O P H O N E E U V W O
X A N D S Y N T H E S I Z E R
```

VIOLA   VIOLIN   XYLOPHONE
CELLO   OBOE   ORGAN
BASS   PICCOLO   CYMBAL
PIANO   TRUMPET   SYNTHESIZER
FLUTE   TUBA   HARP
BANJO   BONGO   WOODBLOCK
GONG   TROMBONE   BASSOON
TRIANGLE   SAXOPHONE   CLARINET
BELL   CASTANETS   GUITAR
   FRENCH HORN   RECORDER

© 1990 by Parker Publishing Company

Name _____ **Date** _____

INSTRUMENT FAMILY PUZZLE

Look at each instrument name below and decide which family it belongs to. Using the following code, write the correct letter next to each instrument:

B = BRASS   S = STRING   P = PERCUSSION   W = WOODWIND

_____ 1. Snare drum

_____ 2. Tuba

_____ 3. Cello

_____ 4. Flute

_____ 5. Guitar

_____ 6. French horn

_____ 7. Castanets

_____ 8. Contrabassoon

_____ 9. Viola

_____ 10. Saxophone

_____ 11. Woodblock

_____ 12. Piano

_____ 13. Bass viol

_____ 14. Xylophone

_____ 15. Bass clarinet

_____ 16. Trumpet

_____ 17. Clarinet

_____ 18. Triangle

_____ 19. Violin

_____ 20. Gong

_____ 21. Oboe

_____ 22. Tambourine

_____ 23. English horn

_____ 24. Maracas

_____ 25. Piccolo

_____ 26. Bongo drum

_____ 27. Harp

_____ 28. Trombone

_____ 29. Cymbals

_____ 30. Bassoon

Name _____   Date _____

INSTRUMENT CROSSWORD PUZZLE

Read the clues at the bottom of this sheet and fill in the crossword puzzle.

ACROSS

1. Instrument slightly larger than a violin
2. Stringed instrument played between the knees
4. Large woodwind instrument called "Clown of the Orchestra"
7. Instrument of the angels
8. Bongo or snare _____
10. Lowest stringed instrument
11. Highest woodwind instrument
12. Lowest brass instrument
13. Keyboard instrument
16. Chopin's major instrument

DOWN

1. A fiddle
2. Woodwind instrument that represented the cat in *Peter and the Wolf*
3. Woodwind instrument that looks like the clarinet
5. The only woodwind instrument that is "gold" or "brass"
6. Oriental percussion instrument
7. French or English _____
9. Instrument similar to a cornet
10. A metal percussion instrument
14. Dixieland stringed instrument
15. Instrument played with mallets

INSTRUMENT RIDDLES

Read each riddle below and write the name of the instrument on the line.

1.   I have 88 keys.   _____

2.   I am a drum that can change pitch.   _____

3.   I was used long ago as a hunting horn.   _____

4.   I sound like a flute, but I am smaller.   _____

5.   I was the cat in *Peter and the Wolf.*   _____

6.   I am the only brass-colored woodwind in-
     strument.   _____

7.   I am used for cadence in marching.   _____

8.   I am used for clicking by Spanish
     dancers.   _____

9.   I am the instrument most like the human
     voice.   _____

10. I am the lowest brass instrument.   _____

11. I am only a few inches bigger than my
     "sister" instrument, the violin.   _____

12. I am a long, silver woodwind instrument.   _____

13. I have a slide.   _____

14. I am the instrument of royalty.   _____

15. I am the lowest stringed instrument.   _____

16. I sit between your knees and am played
     with a bow.   _____

17. I am sometimes called the "Clown of the
     Orchestra."   _____

18. I tune the orchestra on A.   _____

19. I am an electronic instrument that can
     imitate all other instruments.   _____

20. I am an Oriental instrument.   _____

TURKEY TUNES: The Bulletin Board

<u>Objective:</u> Students will improve their sight-reading skills through daily sequential practice.

<u>Materials Needed:</u>

> Light yellow background paper
> Construction paper (brown, red, orange)
> Scissors
> Straight pins
> Felt-tip markers

<u>Construction Directions:</u>

1. Use an opaque projector or transparency to trace the lettering onto orange construction paper. Attach the cut-out letters to the background with straight pins.
2. Draw the staff onto the background with a black felt-tip pen.
3. Trace and cut out eighteen brown turkey bodies and one white turkey body. Use the pattern shown.
4. Use pleated paper fans for tails and wings.
5. Attach the turkeys to the staff with straight pins.

TURKEY TUNES

TURKEY TUNES: Unit Activities

The "Turkey Tunes" illustrated on this bulletin board are not actually Thanksgiving songs. They are called "Turkey Tunes" because the note heads are made in the shape of turkeys. They are simple songs that students can learn to sight read. Only a few measures of each song are included, but the songs are so familiar that two measures should be enough for students to recognize the melody. The teacher may want to choose more advanced songs for older students, remembering to be sure that students are very familiar with the tunes. Each day the songs may be changed, and students may use the bulletin board to practice sight reading.

Sight-reading can be fun as well as a challenge when introduced with this bulletin board. Often the important skills of sight-reading are overlooked in the music classroom. As with most musical skills, it is necessary to reinforce sight-reading skills frequently or they will be forgotten. It is not enough to do a unit on sight-reading and expect students to become proficient. Some form of sight-reading should be practiced every week if skills are to be advanced. It is also important for teachers to evaluate their students' skill levels. If upper grade students have not been exposed to sight-reading, they must start at the beginning. They will fail if the lessons presented are too advanced. The lessons and suggestions presented in this unit first deal with beginning rhythms and advance to more complicated triplets and sixteenth note rhythms. Notes are introduced later, using the Kodály theory of presentation. These lessons may begin at any grade level and advance as students progress. Concepts are built gradually, because a strong foundation is necessary and they depend on a great deal of review.

QUARTERS AND RESTS

The most logical place to begin teaching sight-reading is with the most common unit of rhythm, the quarter note, and its counterpart, the quarter rest. Quarter notes and rests should be presented in many different activities and examples. "Ta" or "quarter" may be used as an oral response. The rest is normally whispered as "rest" or gestured as a place of silence in the music. After demonstrating the correct response, additional examples must be provided for students to do on their own, or they are not truly sight-reading. Whatever method is used, be consistent and insist upon the correct response before moving to the next example. In all examples that follow use a five-step method of presentation.

1. Introduce the new sight-reading note or rhythm by demonstrating it to the class.

2. Have the class try similar examples together.

3. Write several examples on the board and see if students can choose the example performed by the teacher.

4. Choose individual students to perform specific examples and ask other students to identify which example was performed.

5. Have several examples for students to sight-read together. It is helpful to choose two or three very good students to be leaders in sight-reading activities.

These five steps may take several lessons to complete. Do not spend more than five or ten minutes sight-reading in each class period, but do be consistent and include it every week.

There are limited ways to use quarter notes and rests in four count examples. The teacher should write various combinations for students to sight-read following the five-step method of presentation.

Students may also enjoy a "long" or "hard" example, such as:

ADDITION OF EIGHTH NOTES

After students have mastered reading of quarter notes and rests, they will be ready to tackle eighth notes. The eighth note may be verbalized as "two-eighth" or "ti-ti." Again, follow the five-step method of presentation in the following examples. Use four or five examples each day and use different examples every lesson.

Write a "hard" example on the board for students to read:

ADDITION OF HALF NOTES

Next in the sequence of note reading is the introduction of the half note. Use verbalization as "half-note" or "ta-a" for sight-reading activities. Start by using only half notes and quarter notes. Gradually add examples including rests and eighth notes. Also, look for lines in song material for students to read in their books. Even though they may not be able to read the rhythm of an entire song, they can often read one line of the song. It is important that students apply their sight-reading ability to the printed page; they will find it a useful tool for learning new music. Choose a few examples for the class to sight-read each day. Make up additional examples as required.

ADDITION OF TRIPLETS

When introducing the triplet, use examples with only quarter notes and trip-lets. Gradually add rests, eighth notes, and then half notes to the examples. Choose a few of the following examples to work on each day using "trip-o-let" or "trip-le-ti" to verbalize. Make up additional examples as needed.

To add variety to sight-reading exercises, notate names. For example:

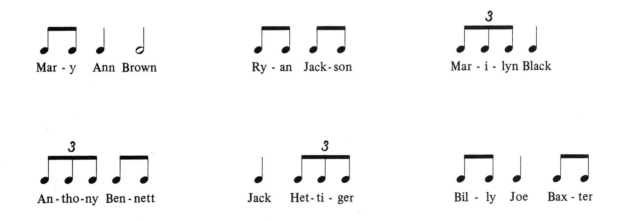

Mar - y   Ann Brown

Ry - an   Jack-son

Mar - i - lyn Black

An - tho-ny Ben -nett

Jack   Het-ti - ger

Bil - ly   Joe   Bax - ter

ADDITION OF DOTTED HALF NOTES

Because the half note has already been introduced, the dotted half note should be easily mastered. Use "half-note-dot" or "ta-a-a" to verbalize. Again, begin with only dotted half notes and quarters and gradually add the other notes. The measures presented here are two measures long to offer more variety.

NURSERY RHYMES

As an extension of sight-reading, have the words of a familiar nursery rhyme on the chalkboard. Have students notate the rhyme. There may be several ways to do each one, so try various rhythms and see which one fits best. Use only rhythms studied so far. Those that fall in 6/8 time should not be tried until those rhythms have been introduced.

"Twinkle, Twinkle Little Star"

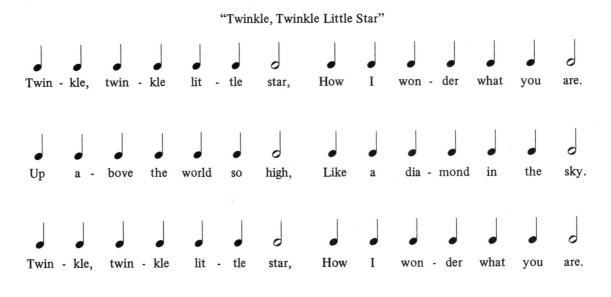

"Lucy Locket"

ADDITION OF SINGLE EIGHTH NOTES

Although eighth notes have already been introduced, the single eighth note is a separate concept. Students must realize that two eighth notes can be written together as 𝅘𝅥𝅮𝅘𝅥𝅮 or separately, as ♪ ♪ . Verbalize single eighth notes as "ti" or "eighth." Use the five-step method of presentation to introduce and practice various examples presented below. The first ten examples are in 4/4 time; the rest are in 6/8 time and include dotted quarter notes and dotted half notes.

Now it is possible to notate songs and rhymes in 6/8 time. For example:

"Hey, Diddle Diddle"

Hey, Did - dle Did - dle, The cat and the fid - dle, The cow jumped o - ver the moon,

The lit - tle dog laughed to see such sport and the dish ran a - way with the spoon.

"Jack and Jill"

Jack and Jill went up the hill to fetch a pail of wa - ter,

Jack fell down and broke his crown and Jill came tum - bling af - ter.

INTRODUCING RESTS

Go back to the appropriate examples and introduce rests in place of the notes. Students should learn to use the eighth rest, half rest and whole rest as well as the quarter rest that was presented in the beginning lesson.

ADDITION OF SIXTEENTH NOTES

Sixteenth notes are the fastest notes that students should try to sight-read. The tempo must remain slow enough to assure the rhythms can be clapped correctly. Use "ti-di-ti-di" or "four sixteenth note" to verbalize rhythms. Choose from the following rhythms or make up others to present on the board for the students to sight-read.

Older students should also learn to count as they clap. After all rhythms are mastered, the teacher should guide third- and fourth-grade students in counting as the rhythms are clapped. Or, try using rhythm instruments as a motivational technique.

SIGHT-READING NOTES

Students must learn to sight-read notes as well as rhythms. Because sight reading rhythms involves only one thought process and reading notes and rhythms together involves a two-thought process, students may be reading very difficult rhythms while reading simple note and rhythm combinations. Notes may be read using letter names, syllables with Kodály hand signals, or numbers. Whichever method is chosen, make sure it is used consistently. Syllables with hand signals will be used in the following examples.

Introduction of Sol and Mi

The first notes to be introduced should be *sol* and *mi*. When beginning, do not use rhythms with the syllables and only concentrate on voice placement. The five-step method of presentation may also be used when introducing notes. Use several examples of sol and mi with different placements on the staff. Also introduce the hand signals.

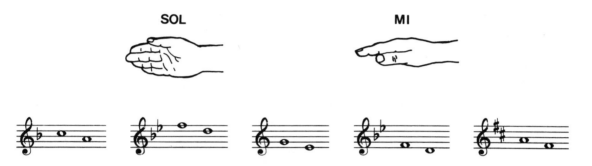

Over the weeks, use several examples of rhythms with sol and mi. Include sight-reading for a *short* period during every class period.

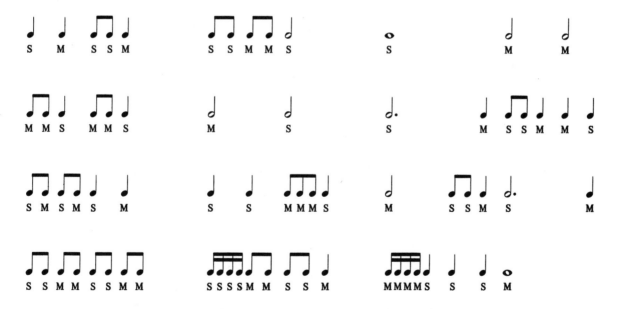

Make up many more examples so students can practice a few new examples each day. Finally, use various placements on the staff with rhythms; begin with easy examples and progress to harder ones. Just a few examples are given here. You should make up new examples every day to keep students in practice. Add new rhythms to examples only when students have mastered old rhythms.

Addition of La

After students have mastered sight-reading sol and mi in several different rhythms and placements on the staff, they are ready to add *la* to their sight-reading skills. Always use the five-step method of presentation when introducing new concepts. It may take many lessons to complete the process, so review of simple examples and repetition play an important part in the development of sight-reading skills.

The hand signal for la is as follows:

LA

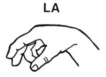

Before sight-reading from a staff, use the hand signal on sol, mi, and la. Lead the class with the hand signals, mixing the order of the notes. You may also let students lead the class using the hand signals.

Next, introduce the notes on the staff without rhythms:

Make up more examples than are listed here, and don't advance to new rhythms until old ones are mastered.

After students are comfortable with notes and rhythms, change the placement of the notes on the staff. Make up many more, similar examples, and don't add new rhythms until the old ones have been mastered.

Addition of Do

When presenting each new note, follow the steps used for the introduction of sol, mi, and la. Here is the hand signal for *do*:

DO

Addition of Re

Follow the steps previously given. Here is the hand signal for *re*:

RE

Addition of Fa

Follow the steps previously explained. Be sure to make up examples as needed. Here is the hand signal for *fa*:

FA

Addition of Ti

Follow all steps previously presented. It will take many years of sight-reading to be able to sight-read songs using the full scale. If students are having difficulties, always go back to a simpler level and review the material. Here is the hand signal for *ti*:

TI

NOVEMBER ANSWER KEY

Instrument Wordsearch

A	V	I	O	L	A	R	C	E	L	L	O	T	S	P
B	I	C	E	I	G	E	H	D	G	F	B	A	S	S
J	O	K	L	M	U	C	P	I	A	N	O	N	O	P
F	L	U	T	E	I	O	I	Q	R	S	E	T	F	C
U	I	V	R	W	T	R	C	X	G	Y	Z	W	R	Y
A	N	T	U	B	A	D	C	E	O	X	C	O	E	M
B	C	D	M	A	R	E	O	F	N	Y	L	O	N	B
H	A	R	P	S	G	R	L	H	G	L	A	D	C	A
I	J	K	E	S	L	B	O	N	G	O	R	B	H	L
M	N	O	T	O	R	G	A	N	B	P	I	L	H	B
P	Q	T	R	O	M	B	O	N	E	H	N	O	O	A
T	R	I	A	N	G	L	E	R	L	O	E	C	R	N
C	A	S	T	A	N	E	T	S	L	N	T	K	N	J
T	S	A	X	O	P	H	O	N	E	E	U	V	W	O
X	A	N	D	S	Y	N	T	H	E	S	I	Z	E	R

Instrument Family Puzzle

1.	P	11.	P	21.	W
2.	B	12.	P	22.	P
3.	S	13.	S	23.	W
4.	W	14.	P	24.	P
5.	S	15.	W	25.	W
6.	B	16.	B	26.	P
7.	P	17.	W	27.	S
8.	W	18.	P	28.	B
9.	S	19.	S	29.	P
10.	W	20.	P	30.	W

Instrument Crossword Puzzle

Across:

1. Viola
2. Cello
4. Bassoon
7. Harp
8. Drum
10. Bass
11. Piccolo
12. Tuba
13. Organ
16. Piano

Down:

1. Violin
2. Clarinet
3. Oboe
5. Saxophone
6. Gong

7. Horn
9. Trumpet
10. Bell
14. Banjo
15. Xylophone

Instrument Riddles

1. Piano
2. Timpani or kettle drum
3. French horn
4. Piccolo
5. Clarinet
6. Saxophone
7. Snare drum
8. Castanets
9. Violin
10. Tuba

11. Viola
12. Flute
13. Trombone
14. Trumpet
15. Bass
16. Cello
17. Bassoon
18. Oboe
19. Synthesizer
20. Gong

December

"Elves and Elements"

"Star Search"

ELVES AND ELEMENTS: The Bulletin Board

Objective: Students will improve their concepts of the elements of music by working with exercises in melody, harmony, rhythm, form, and tone color.

Materials Needed:

Light green background paper
Construction paper (red, dark green, skin-tone, yellow, blue)
Felt-tip markers
Scissors
Straight pins
Glue

Construction Directions:

1. Use an opaque projector or transparency to trace the lettering onto the red construction paper. Attach the cut-out letters to the background with straight pins.
2. Trace the elves' clothing with black marker onto dark green construction paper.
3. Trace the elves' faces and hands onto skin-tone construction paper.
4. Trace the balls onto colored construction paper. Add lettering of elements with a black felt-tip pen.
5. Cut out all figures and attach to the board with straight pins. Pull the figures away from the board to give a three-dimensional effect.

ELVES AND ELEMENTS: Unit Activities

This December bulletin board features elves building balls which represent the elements of music. Because the elements of music are the building materials of composition, it is appropriate to visualize them in the construction of balls. This metaphor will help students to visualize the use of elements in the music they sing, play, compose, and hear. Even beginning students should become familiar with the proper terms when discussing music.

Several activities are explained in detail for each element. The class may be divided into four groups, with each group at a center participating in the activities together. The activities may also be used as group tasks for the entire class. Each day when listening or singing, have individual students go to the bulletin board and point to an element. Each student should discuss that particular composition and explain how the element he is pointing to is used in the music. If time is limited, choose only one element that is obvious in a particular composition for discussion.

ELVES AND ELEMENTS

RHYTHM

FORM

HARMONY

TONE COLOR

MELODY

MELODY

1. Sing several melodies appropriate to each grade level.

2. Listen to melodies and determine whether they are high, low, go up, go down, or stay the same.

3. Show melodic direction (up, down, same) with hands as students sing simple songs.

4. Sing a simple song and have students draw melodic direction on the board or on paper:

   "Hot Cross Buns"

5. Using any keyboard instrument, have students play a melody going up, going down, staying the same.

6. Have students make up a song and sing it. Write it down in notation so they can see what it "looks like."

7. Make up different words to melodies.

8. Make up a pentatonic song and have students accompany with a melody on the bells. (Use only the black notes on a keyboard.)

9. While listening to a recording, ask, "What instrument is playing the melody?"

10. Frequently, ask questions about the music students are singing from their books: "On which staff does the melody go up?" "Does the song end high or low?" "How many notes stay the same at the beginning of the song?" "Which two lines of the melody are alike?"

RHYTHM

1. Lead the class in echo clapping.

2. Have students take rhythmic dictation beginning with quarter and eighth notes. They should do it together as a class first; later, try having students take dictation individually.

3. Notate names in the classroom.

4. Ask questions about rhythms on a printed page: "Which staff has two quarter notes?" "How many eighth notes are in the second staff?" "How many half notes are in the song?" "Which two staves have rhythms that are alike?"

5. Accompany songs with various rhythm instruments. Notate simple patterns for students to play.

6. Sight-read rhythmic patterns. (Refer to November's "Turkey Tunes.")

7. Make up color pages where pictures are marked with rhythms for various colors:

$\downarrow$ = Red $\downarrow$ = Green $\downarrow\downarrow$ = Blue   o = Black

8. List rhythm patterns on the chalkboard. Clap a pattern and see if the students can choose the correct example.

9. Use movement activities in which students move to music on quarter notes, eighth notes, half notes, etc.

10. For students in the early grades, use movement songs with claps, taps, snaps, bends, body sounds, etc.

TONE COLOR

1. Name instruments by sight. Begin with classroom instruments and advance to pictures of orchestra instruments.

2. Name instruments by sound. Play classroom instruments while students are not looking. Also, have students identify instruments from recordings.

3. Play a game where someone is "it." One person speaks and the one who is "it" has to identify the correct person. This demonstrates voice timbre.

4. Classify classroom instruments into categories (ringing, shaking, banging, etc.).

5. Listen to *Peter and the Wolf.*

6. Name animals and have students select instruments that would be appropriate for that animal (elephant—drums, tuba, or bassoon; bird—flute, bells, high notes on piano).

7. Have students close their eyes and try to name all the sounds they heard.

8. Use an electronic keyboard to demonstrate various sounds.

9. Visit a band or orchestra rehearsal or concert and talk about the instruments.

10. Have high-school or upper-elementary students come to the classroom and demonstrate instruments.

FORM

1. Practice identifying phrases or "places where the music feels like stopping."

2. Listen to music and identify similar and different sections.

3. Use various actions to a section of a song so students can "watch" the form (A = Clap   B = Snap fingers   C = Bend knees   D = Hands over head, etc.)

4. Display colored sheets of paper with four figures representing four phrases in a song (triangles, bells, squares, etc.). Students draw the shapes according to the form of the song. Use songs with four short phrases to begin.

5. Have students identify similar and different sections on a page of printed music.

6. Divide class into four groups and give each group a different color of construction paper. Have each group stand and hold up their papers when the corresponding phrase of music is played.

    A. "Twinkle Twinkle Little Star"—*aba* or red-green-red

    B. "Hot Cross Buns"—*aaba* or red-red-green-red

    C. "Skip to My Lou"—*abac* or red-green-red-blue

7. Sing familiar songs and list their forms on the board.

8. Give four choices on the board for the form of a song. See if students can choose the correct one.

9. Listen to a rondo and write the form on the board for students to follow *(abacada)*.

10. Have four students each make up and play a phrase on the "black notes" of bells (pentatonic). Make up songs using these four phrases in various forms *(abab, abcd, abca, abacada)*.

HARMONY

1. Play a simple melody line on the piano. Play a harmony part with the melody. Let students describe the difference between the two sounds.

2. Listen to music that is sung in harmony.

3. Chant words with different rhythms together. Divide the class into three parts and choose words according to seasons:

Eas - ter Time   Bun - ny Rab - bit   Egg   Hunt

4. Have the class sing simple songs with ostinato patterns.

5. Have the class sing various combinations of notes together (sol-mi, mi-do, do-sol, do-fa, do-la, etc).

6. Sing partner songs.

7. Play chords on the autoharp or on the resonator bells.

8. Play various two-note combinations on bells or Orff instruments.

9. Play ostinato patterns on soprano, alto, tenor, and bass Orff instruments to accompany songs.

10. Discuss major, minor, and pentatonic scales. Have students listen to examples and decide whether they are major, minor, or pentatonic.

ELEMENT CENTERS

The following activities are designed to be used as centers with four groups working at various centers at the same time. They can also be used as group activities for the class. It is helpful to show films such as "Hello, I'm Music" by EMC Corporation or to discuss each musical element before beginning the activities. The class should be divided into four groups with each group sitting in a separate row. Try to have a band or piano student in each group so they can help students having difficulties. The teacher will explain all the four centers and then assign each group to a center. They will have 7-10 minutes to go to a center and complete the task. Groups must work quietly because four activities are occurring simultaneously. Any student causing trouble should return to his seat. At the end of 7-10 minutes "time" is called and *all* students return to their seats. The teacher assigns the four groups to a different center. This procedure is followed until all groups have completed the tasks at all centers. When paper and pencil are needed, have them available at centers. Be sure to count pencils after each group moves.

Melody Center

Melody Puzzles

This center will have envelopes containing melody puzzles. There should be one complete staff with a melody and another staff cut into pieces in each envelope. Students must arrange the pieces to match the completed staff. They may trade puzzles and work as many as they can before "time" is called. Make sure students put all pieces back in the correct envelopes before trading puzzles. Here is an example:

Scale Center

This center should be set up outside in the hall, if possible. A set of bells and a sheet with the following scales written on it should be available:

1. Major
2. Minor
3. Pentatonic
4. Chromatic

Students should leave the room one at a time and play the four scales. Station a band or piano student in the hall to aid students who may have trouble. Students may leave their seats and go into the hall one at a time at this center. This will eliminate noise problems in the hall. When everyone is finished they must wait in their seats until "time" is called. If the row is moving too slowly, the teacher should send the next person out.

Playing Melodies on Bells

Place sets of bells around the room for each student. If there are not enough bells available, students may work in pairs. Have familiar melodies such as "Mary Had a Little Lamb," "Hot Cross Buns," or "Jingle Bells" written out at each set of bells. It is not necessary to have the entire song. Have the note names written under the notes. Students should go to a set of bells, play the song, then move to a different set of bells with a different song. They should play as many songs as they can until "time" is called. They *must* play softly, because there may be many people playing at the same time.

Write a Melody

Students will pick up a pencil and a paper with a single staff on it. The students then follow instructions written on the board:

1. Draw a treble clef.
2. Use 4/4 time signature.
3. Divide the staff into five or more measures.
4. Put four counts in each measure.
5. End on C.

After "time" has been called and students are back in their seats, the teacher should play the songs on the piano. Even though they are single melody lines it is possible to add harmony as the melody is played. Students are always very proud of their compositions and enjoy hearing them played. (Students must have previous experience at writing music in order to be able to be successful at this activity center.)

Rhythm Center

Dice Game

Either buy musical dice with rhythms or make a set. These can be made of wood with rhythms printed on each of the six sides.

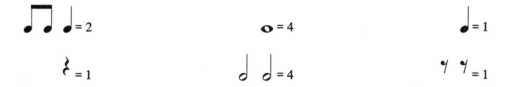

Students should have the dice and a paper telling the values of the rhythms.

Students sit in a circle on the floor. The first person throws the dice and counts his score. The next person throws and the game continues. The person with the most points when "time" is called is the winner.

Rhythm Composition

Have the board divided into eight measures, or one measure for each person in the group. Students are to come to the board and fill in their measure with four counts and then sit on the front row of seats. The teacher must work with this center as she hands out various rhythm instruments to the group. The group plays the rhythm composition as the teacher counts. The composition may be played several times with students exchanging instruments each time.

Counting Worksheet

Students take a sheet of paper with rhythms written in various time signatures. They are to write counts under the notes. The examples must be kept short for students to be able to finish when "time" is called.

The teacher could check the first person finished and have that person check everyone else in the group.

Rhythm Flash Cards

Prepare flash cards by writing large rhythms with magic marker on one side of the paper and small rhythms with counts on the back of the paper.

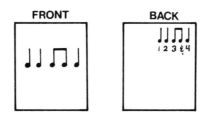

Prepare twenty to twenty-five cards. Choose a leader for the group and have that person show the cards. The first person in the group must try to clap the rhythm. If he can clap it, he gets the cards. If he cannot, the leader goes to the next person. The game continues, and the person with the most cards is the winner and gets to be the leader as the cards are shown again.

Tone-Color Center

Hearing Identification

Make a tape recording of ten different instruments for students to identify by sound. Each student will need a paper and pencil to complete the task. As the tape is played students write the names of the correct instruments. Give the answers at the end of the tape so students can check themselves.

Matching Sounds

Prepare twelve small containers such as L'eggs panty-hose eggs or margarine tubs, and put various items in each so that there are six sets of matching containers (two with sand, two with rocks, two with grass, etc.). Students must shake containers and match the sounds inside. Make sure containers are taped shut so that students can't look inside and so the lids won't fly off when they are shaken. The teacher should check to see if matches are correct when "time" is called.

Sounds Around

Provide each student with a pencil and paper. Usually quarter sheets of paper left in stacks are big enough for most centers, and eight pencils are adequate. Instruct students to list as many sounds as they can hear. They may list sounds they hear inside or outside the room. The person with the longest list is the winner.

Instrument Identification

Because tone color may involve instruments of the orchestra, students should be able to recognize instruments by sight. Have ten to twelve pictures of instruments hanging on the wall. Students will need pencil and paper so they can write down the name of each instrument. The teacher should check the papers or call off names of instruments so students can check their own papers.

Form Center

Same or Different?

Prepare a tape recording of ten pairs of short melodies. The second melody in the pair should be the "same" or "different" from the first melody. Students must write "S" for "same" and "D" for "different" as they listen to the pairs of melodies. Include the answers at the end of the tape so students can check themselves.

Identification of Form

List five page numbers of a music text on the board. Each of these pages should have a four-line song with a very obvious form. Students should have a book, pencil, and paper. They must look up the page number and write the form of each song. The teacher should check papers when the group is finished.

Compose ABA Song

The teacher should pass out papers printed with three staffs. Each staff should have four measures, and the time signature should be 4/4. Instruct students to write a song with the first and last lines alike and the middle line different. Ask them to be sure four counts are in each measure and to end on C. The teacher may check songs when "time" is called, or play them on the piano. (Students should have had previous experience writing songs before attempting to complete this task individually. More accomplished students may help students having difficulty.)

Boogie Pattern

A very obvious form is the "boogie" pattern. Help students play the following boogie pattern on the piano:

Write letter names under the notes and write the letter names in pencil on the keys of the piano. They will wipe off with a damp cloth. The teacher should sit in the middle with a student on each end of the piano. Explain the pattern as skipping, going up by steps, and coming back down. Play the pattern slowly, calling out letter names. Let the students on each end play together, going slowly and pausing when needed. Let those two students go back to the group and two more come to the piano to play the boogie. All students in the group can gather around the piano so they can see.

Harmony Center

Writing Chords

Staff paper and pencils should be available at this center. As an introduction, explain that a chord is two or more notes sounded together. To be sounded together the notes must be written on top of each other on the staff. Ask students to try chords on lines, some on spaces, some on lines and spaces together, some spread apart, some close together, etc. Draw some chords on the board as examples. Let students write chords on their staff paper. When "time" is called, play chords that students have written.

Experimental Chord Center

In one area of the room place a set of resonator bells that can be individually removed from the box. Choose one student to be in charge of the center. The other group members must stand in a line, and only the leader may handle the bells. The leader follows written instructions for handing out the bells and experimenting with harmony. The leader hands out the first three bells to the first three students and then says, "One, two, ready, go." Those three people play together eight times. The leader puts those bells away and hands the next three bells to the next three people. The leader always says, "One, two, ready, go," and the group always plays eight times together. The leader should hand out bells as follows:

1. Three bells in a row—CDE
2. Three bells that skip—CEG
3. Bells to make a seventh chord—CEGB♭
4. Bells for D Major chord—DF♯A
5. Bells for a minor chord—ACE
6. Let group choose any three bells to form a chord cluster

Singing in Two Parts

The teacher must work with this group. Divide the group into two parts. Sing a round, such as "Are You Sleeping" or "Row, Row, Row Your Boat." Ask students to listen to the harmony as they sing. Change parts and try the round again. Divide the group into three parts. Have students sing the following harmonies together. Start with the low note and add other notes until all three are sounding together: do-mi-sol, do-fa-la, re-sol-ti, mi-sol-do (high).

Chord on Autoharp

This center should be outside in the hall if possible. Have a simple song with chords written out at the autoharp. Only two students may go to this center at a time to cut down on noise. Both students must sing together, and they take turns playing the autoharp. When each has had a turn playing the autoharp, they return to the room so the next two students can go out. Make sure no one stays out too long so everyone in the group gets a turn.

STAR SEARCH: The Bulletin Board

Objective: Students will improve their performing abilities by presenting a program.

Materials Needed:

Dark blue background paper
Construction paper (black, yellow, light green, skin-tone)
Light green tissue paper
Foil (silver, gold)
Silver glitter
Scissors
Straight pins
Glue
Felt-tip marker
Photos of students

Construction Directions:

1.   Use the yellow background paper for the sign "Star Search." Cut out black letters and pin them onto the yellow sign. Place gold and silver foil in pleated or ruffled fashion around the yellow sign. Sprinkle with glitter.

2.   On silver foil, trace the star shape and angel figure with black felt-tip pen. Cut out a hole for the face (to put in the students' pictures). Cut out and attach the figures to the background with pins.

3.   Trace and cut green tissue paper for the elf and red tissue paper for the dancer. Puff out and ruffle the elf's and dancer's clothing for a three-dimensional effect as they are pinned to the board. Use skin-tone construction paper for the hands and feet of the figures. Use the students' photos to fill in the faces.

STAR SEARCH: Unit Activities

The holiday season is usually a time of concerts, musicals, and other performances. If a musical is being presented, characters from that musical could be used for this bulletin board. Perhaps students could bring a large picture from home to place in the face of the character for which they have been chosen. If a small school picture is used, draw a face for the character and place the picture below the face of the character.

It is important for students to learn to perform in front of audiences. This will be a time of year when songs are "polished," try-outs are held, and leading roles

STAR SEARCH

and soloists are chosen. A lot of energy goes into a successful holiday production. It can be a very exciting time of year. Activities in this unit guide the teacher in searching for talent and helping students to become better performers. The "Star Search" theme may be used year 'round on a small section of the bulletin board. The teacher may choose a "Student of the Week" or "Student of the Month." That student's picture would be placed in the star for the appropriate time.

USING THE MICROPHONE

All students should become accustomed to using a microphone. They are fascinated by the microphone and love experimenting with it—even though they may be timid about using it. If the teacher works with the microphone several times during the year, then students will be ready when it is time to give an important program. The teacher should make the following explanation or a similar one before allowing students to use the microphone.

> "Every one of you will probably have to use a microphone some time. Many times I see adults who do not know how to use microphones properly. Often they don't get close enough to the microphone for it to pick up the sound. [Demonstrate the proper distance.] Also, it's important to speak into it from the proper angle. Speak directly into the microphone, not to one side of it. [Demonstrate correct and incorrect angle.] Sometimes people back away from the microphone because they are startled by the sound of their voice. The microphone does change your voice, because it is electronically amplified. If you are familiar with how your voice sounds on the microphone, you will not be startled."

Students should then take turns speaking into the microphone. Even small children can practice by announcing their names, addresses, hobbies, etc. You should stand beside them, giving directions if they are having trouble. If students are holding the microphone instead of walking up to it on a stand, you should warn them about getting too close to the amplifier and causing feedback. Demonstrate this to the students.

After the students have had several chances to talk into the microphone, they will be ready to sing into it. First, ask for volunteers. This will encourage the rest of the class. Choose a simple song and have individual students sing the verse with everyone else singing the chorus together. Choose songs with many verses, such as "Skip to My Lou," "Yankee Doodle," or "Sweet Betsy from Pike." Eventually, all students should sing with the microphone. Hesitant students will usually be encouraged if the entire class is in a line and each student takes a short turn.

SING SOLOS

Some students are eager to sing solos, while others are hesitant to sing alone. Activities with echo singing beginning in the early grades will encourage students to not be shy in later years. Often, going down the line with everyone sing-ing an echo or short verse is the best method. Students know they must take their turn and after a few times it seems routine that everyone should sing a solo. Any negative comments from students cannot be tolerated; even criticism from you should not be given in the early stages of solo singing. Sometimes it is best to start singing in quartets, then trios, duets, and finally solo. This gives students time to adjust to the situation gradually. It is not necessary to stand in front of the class, so students can be more comfortable singing from their seats. Once solo singing is accepted in the class, try singing with the microphone.

TALENT DAY

A day set aside for students to perform can be very enlightening. This gives students an outlet to be creative, and you may find students with talents of which you were unaware. The day should be announced two weeks in advance, and stu-dents may prepare something in groups or by themselves. This can be any kind of performance—twirling, dancing, singing, playing an instrument, chants, poems, etc. It is a voluntary activity, and it should be very informal. On the as-signed day, you should ask students to raise their hands if they have anything special to do. At first, only a few may have something prepared, so you may need to have a lesson plan prepared to fill the class period. As the activity is repeated, more students will want to perform. In upper grades, Talent Day might be more formal, with students performing in front of others.

PUPPET PLAYS

Working with puppets gives students many opportunities. Writing their own skits—or making them up as they go along—provides a creative avenue. Stu-dents who are shy about singing solos may do so if it is the puppet performing in-stead of themselves. It is also an extension for performing and acting.

Students may bring puppets from home, or simple ones may be made from socks and magic markers and scissors. Divide students up into groups and let them prepare a puppet skit using a song or holiday theme as the subject. They should take turns presenting their performances to the class. The audience should discuss rules concerning attending a performance. These rules should be listed on the board and followed as each group performs:

A. Don't talk.
B. Don't wriggle or leave seats.
C. Focus attention on the performers.

CRITIQUE PERFORMANCES

For students to become better performers they should have experience cri-tiquing various performances. The teacher may record different classes singing a song, and the class can discuss good points and bad points of each performance. It is also beneficial to videotape past performances so students can watch and offer comments. Young students will just raise their hands and discuss, but older students may write a paper offering suggestions, pointing out weaknesses, or comparing two performances. Some points to consider are as follows:

Musical

1. Costuming
2. Stage set
3. Do performers face audience?
4. Are performers loud enough?
5. Are characters believable?
6. Which characters were best? Why?

Concert

1. Did performers get on risers with uniformity?
2. Did performers stand straight with no wriggling or talking?
3. Were entrances and cutoffs together?
4. Were voices blended?
5. Were performers on the correct parts?
6. Did performers know their music well?
7. Was the tone light and not forced?
8. Were vowels and consonants handled properly?
9. Were performers sharp or flat?
10. Were songs performed with expression (dynamics, tempo changes, etc.)?

TRYOUTS

Tryouts are a necessary evil in every play or musical. Usually you are familiar enough with students' abilities to limit the selection to a few students. Still, every student should have the opportunity to audition, and some may surprise you. It is most important to go into the tryouts with an open mind. Tryouts may be held during class time or before or after school. Usually for a play, the audition will consist of reading a portion of the play and singing a familiar song. It is important to make a decision quickly because building up hope over several weeks magnifies the disappointment of not being chosen for a part. It is also a good idea to check with the classroom teacher. Those students who may be very talented may also not be very dependable. When auditioning parts for a musical, have all the characters listed. Beside each character's name, notes should be made ("many solos to sing," "large character part," "no speaking lines"). Students may try for specific parts, or just audition by reading and singing and let you assign parts. Sometimes, it is best to have a first audition to limit parts to two or three of the best students. Then a second audition is held with a panel of teachers making the final selections.

STUDY OF MUSICAL PERFORMANCES

To aid students in performing, you should make them aware of great performances. An appropriate choice for December would be *The Nutcracker*.

There are many records, filmstrips, and videotapes of *The Nutcracker*. Usually, it is performed some time during the holiday season on television. Lead students in a discussion of ballet. Help male students realize that this is not just "girl stuff." A male ballet dancer is actually an athlete with tremendous muscle coordination and strength. Have books available on ballet so students may read or give reports on the subject.

Use *The Nutcracker* worksheet as a listening guide or testing device for older students. For younger students, select some of the questions to lead them through a listening experience and discussion.

STEPS FOR PRESENTING A MUSICAL

A great deal of preparation goes into presenting a musical. The preparation begins with preliminary steps taken by the teacher long before the class begins rehearsal. The teacher should know the music, characters, and staging thoroughly before beginning. The following steps should be taken as a musical is prepared.

1. List all characters in the musical. Make notes for each one ("Long speaking parts," "Solos to sing," "Only speaks four times," "Acting song," etc.).

2. List all songs in the musical. Again make notes for reference ("Chorus only," "Jack's solo," "Difficult with high parts," etc.).

3. Tape all solos. Make a practice tape for each character with solo parts. One tape may have five solos and another only one. This is an invaluable tool when parts are assigned. Every cast member can take a tape home and learn all of his or her solos at home.

4. Read and play songs from the musical until they are thoroughly familiar.

5. List all scenes and props that will be needed. Draw pictures of the scenes or blocks for where all furniture and props will be set on stage.

6. List the characters and what costumes they will need. If parents are preparing costumes, give them an idea of what is needed and let them do the major planning in this area. Work closely with them so costuming fits the characters' style.

7. Hold auditions and assign parts.

8. Begin holding rehearsals with two or three characters at a time. Work on solos and check individuals for memorization of their parts. Also work on any choreography.

9. Announce what props are needed and let students begin bringing them in.

10. Assign someone to take care of props. Assign another crew for scene changes, someone to pull curtains, to prompt lines, lighting, accompanist, etc.

11. Begin rehearsing complete scenes. The entire cast might not still be present. Try to have props available, even though it may not be possible to practice in the place where the musical will eventually be performed.

12. Practice with the entire cast and all special crew members. Start in plenty of time to work on problems. With all the preliminary work, everything should go well at this point. Always make lists of things that need attention.

13. Have a dress rehearsal.

14. Give the final performance.

PLACES TO PERFORM

Once a performing group is ready, it is necessary that it have a place to perform. The group might be a musical cast, a choral group, a small ensemble, or a few soloists, and it is up to you to search out possibilities for performance spaces. This will not only give students more performing experience, but it will also be a public relations opportunity for the music program. Some possibilities for places to perform include:

1. Evening performances (concerts or musicals) for the community

2. Performances before the entire student body

3. Small-group performances in front of individual classes

4. A district festival, inviting other schools to perform and attend

5. A concert taped for radio broadcast

6. Performances for PTA meetings

7. Performances at nursing homes

8. Performances at service organizations (such as the Lions or Elks)

9. Caroling or singing at Christmas parties

10. Benefit performances in the community

Name _____ Date _____

THE NUTCRACKER SUITE

Part One: General Information

1. The name of the little girl is _____.
2. The girl receives a _____ as a gift.
3. The toy becomes _____ during a struggle between the little girl and her brother.
4. The girl goes to sleep and dreams that the _____ and _____ fight.
5. She throws her _____ and kills the _____ _____.
6. The Prince takes the girl to his many different_____.
7. The _____ _____ Fairy dances for them.
8. The musical instruments called _____ dance for them.
9. The _____ dance a waltz for them.
10. The girl wakes up and finds everything was a _____.

Part Two: "Overture"

1. The first solo is:
   a. Drum   b. Trumpet   c. Flute
2. The middle section is played by:
   a. Brass   b. Strings   c. Percussion
3. This music is:
   a. Depressing   b. Happy   c. Sad

Part Three: "March"

1. Two families of instruments alternate at the beginning. They are:
   a. Brass/Strings   b. Woodwinds/Strings   c. Percussion/Brass
2. The middle section is:
   a. Faster than the beginning   b. Slower than the beginning
3. The form of the music is:
   a. ABC   b. ABA   c. AAB

Part Four: "Dance of the Sugar Plum Fairy"

1. At the beginning the music is:
   a. Loud   b. Fast   c. Soft
2. The melody is played by:
   a. Trumpets   b. Celesta   c. French horn
3. The last part of the melody in the song is:
   a. Higher   b. Lower   c. Slower

Part Five: "Trepak"

1. What country does this represent?
   a. America   b. Spain   c. Russia
2. The music is:
   a. Peaceful   b. Quiet   c. Wild and furious
3. What instruments play?
   a. All families   b. Strings   c. Percussion

Part Six: "Chinese Dance"

1. What instrument plays the melody?
   a. Clarinets   b. Flutes   c. Strings
2. The music is:
   a. Light   b. Wild and furious   c. Heavy and low
3. The strings play in the beginning:
   a. Loudly   b. Pizzicato   c. Bowed

Part Seven: "Dance of the Flutes"

1. The music moves in:
   a. Duple meter   b. Triple meter
2. Is the first theme repeated?
   a. Yes   b. No
3. What instruments play the main theme?
   a. Tubas   b. Bassoons   c. Flutes

Part Eight: "Waltz of the Flowers"

1. What stringed instrument plays the introduction?
   a. Violin   b. Harp   c. Bass
2. The music moves in:
   a. Duple meter   b. Triple meter
3. The melody gets:
   a. Higher   c. Lower

DECEMBER ANSWER KEY

The Nutcracker Suite

Part One: General Information

1. Clara or Marie
2. Nutcracker
3. broken
4. toys; mice
5. slipper; Mouse King

6. lands (or kingdoms)
7. Sugar Plum
8. flutes
9. flowers
10. dream

Part Two: "Overture"

1. c   2. b   3. b

Part Three: "March"

1. a   2. a   3. a

Part Four: "Dance of the Sugar Plum Fairy"

1. c   2. b   3. a

Part Five: "Trepak"

1. c   2. c   3. a

Part Six: "Chinese Dance"

1. b   2. a   3. b

Part Seven: "Dance of the Flutes"

1. a   2. a   3. c

Part Eight: "Waltz of the Flowers"

1. b   2. b   3. a

January

"Chugging into the New Year"

"Frosty Folk Music"

CHUGGING INTO THE NEW YEAR: The Bulletin Board

Objective: Students will improve their knowledge of dynamics by learning songs that illustrate dynamics; they will apply these dynamic markings to song material.

Materials Needed:

Light blue background paper
Construction paper (black, white, various other colors)
Yarn (black and grey)
Scissors
Straight pins
Glue
Felt-tip markers

Construction Directions:

1. Use an opaque projector or transparency to trace the lettering onto the black construction paper. Attach the cut-out letters with straight pins to the background paper.
2. Use yarn to make the steam from the train and the tracks.
3. Trace the engine onto dark blue paper and give it black wheels. Cut out and arrange the engine on the tracks with pins. Make the other cars of the train in various colors.
4. Trace the animal patterns onto white paper and color in with felt markers. Make twelve black construction paper wheels.
5. Decorate the tops of the wagons with various colors of construction paper.
6. Attach the animals and wagons to the board with pins. Glue yarn over the animals for the bars.
7. Use black construction paper for the dynamic letters and attach them over the cages with pins.

CHUGGING INTO THE NEW YEAR: Unit Activities

As students return from vacation, this bright bulletin board will remind them that the school year is moving on and it's time to get to work. Any unit could be portrayed in the boxcars; a unit on dynamics has been shown here. Association with the animals will help students remember the dynamic levels. Young students will have color and drawing activities, while older students will participate in advanced activities to reinforce their knowledge of dynamics. Dynamics should be introduced in kindergarten, and reinforcement activities must be practiced every year to assure students use dynamic levels properly. Let students change animals on the bulletin board daily as long as the animal represents the level of dynamic sound.

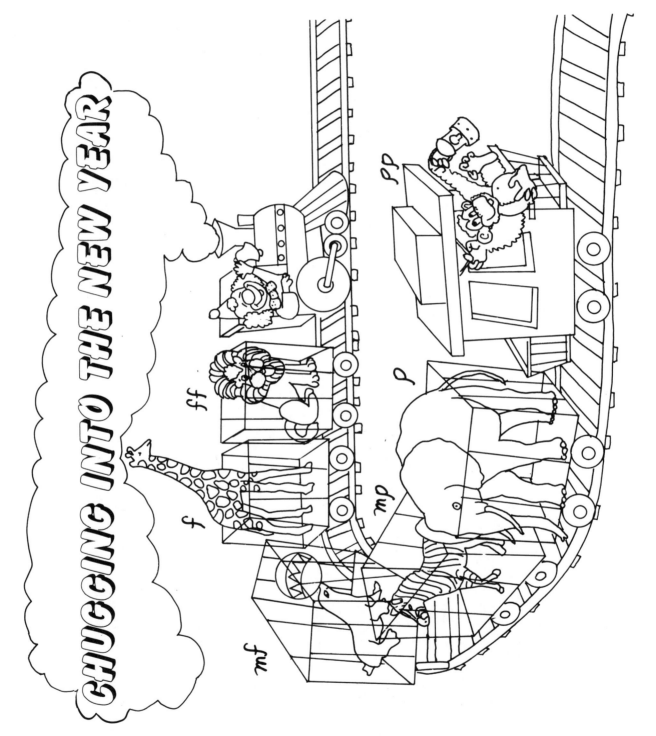

CHUGGING INTO THE NEW YEAR

DYNAMIC POSTER CONTEST

Lead students in a discussion of other animals that could be used for each dynamic level instead of the animal pictured in the train. It will probably be easier to limit levels to "soft" and "loud." Various degrees in between are hard to identify. Pass out construction paper and choose a level (soft or loud). Let students draw and color an animal of their choice to represent the dynamic level. Display all animal pictures so students can see the possibilities and associate these animals with the proper level. Choose one picture to be the "winner" and display it in a special place. Students love contests, and if this is announced before the activities begin, it will add excitement to the project. A special ribbon or prize could be given for the winner.

EXPERIMENTING WITH DYNAMICS

Take familiar songs and try different dynamic levels to see which works best. This can be done at any grade level, depending on the selection of song material.

"Twinkle, Twinkle Little Star"

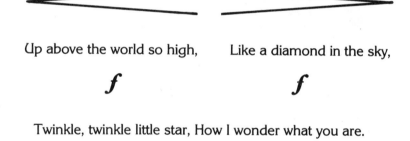

Twinkle, twinkle little star,   How I wonder what you are.

Up above the world so high,   Like a diamond in the sky,

f   *f*

Twinkle, twinkle little star, How I wonder what you are.

Have the words to a song printed on the chalkboard so all students can see. Have a student come to the board and mark in dynamic levels above the words. Sing the song using the dynamic levels as they have been written in. Erase those dynamics and have a different student mark different dynamics above the words. Sing the song again using the new dynamic levels. Do this several times and then decide as a class which sounds best. Sing the song using these dynamics.

LISTENING AND LABELING DYNAMICS

Give each student a half sheet of paper and a pencil. Play ten different recordings that are either loud or soft. Here are some examples you might use:

Soft

Hansel and Gretel Overture by Humperdinck

Theme and variation, *Surprise Symphony*, No. 94, Second Movement, by Haydn

First movement, *Symphony No. 9* by Dvořák

Third movement, *Symphony No. 4* by Tchaikovsky

Second movement, *Symphony No. 8* by Beethoven

Loud

Minuet from *Symphony No. 40* by Mozart

Hoedown by Copland

First movement of *Piano Concerto* by Grieg

Fourth movement of *Symphony No. 3* by Saint-Saëns

Finale of *Overture to William Tell* by Rossini

Students should label each of the ten examples either *p* or *f*. Be sure to use examples that are obviously loud or soft. Labeling dynamics using *pp*, *mp*, *mf*, or *ff* may be done as an advanced exercise. It is hard to grade this degree of dynamic level and disputes may arise between choices. You may give an opinion, but no one can really say how loud *mf* or *f* is. For this reason, it may be best to limit the activity to *p* and *f*.

DYNAMIC RACE

Each student must have paper and pencil for this race. When "time" begins students must look through their music text books and list examples of dynamic markings. They must list the marking and page number of the song. When time is called (ten minutes), the person with the most examples is the winner. The winner of the game should read aloud each page number and the dynamic level that is on the page. All the other students should find the page and check to see that the winner is correct. This not only checks the winner, but it reinforces the concept of dynamic levels as students find the markings on the printed page.

PLAYING WITH DYNAMICS

Pass out rhythm instruments to an entire class or to a group of students in the class. Have a simple rhythm pattern printed on the board. Students in upper grades may also use this activity if a more complicated rhythmic phrase is used. Example:

Write in a dynamic marking above the rhythmic phrase. In this example it's *p*. Have students play the example softly. This is a good exercise for stressing various degrees of dynamic levels. Next erase the marking and write *pp* instead. Announce to students, "We played the example softly before. Now we're going to play it *pianissimo*, which is even softer." (Play example *pp*.) Play the example again at the piano level. Announce to students, "We just played piano again. Now see if you can play just a little louder for *mezzo piano*." (Play example. If students do not play it at the correct level, try again.) Try each level until all of the following have been mastered:

pp   *p*   *mp*   *mf*   *f*   *ff*

Finally, have all dynamic levels listed on the board as they are above. Point to a level and see if students can play at that dynamic level. Skip around on the list so students must remember and associate each level in order to play it correctly. If students play too loudly for a particular level, have them repeat it until it is correct. The teacher may say something like "That is too loud for *mp*. There's not enough difference between *ff* and *mp* the way you played it. Try again a little more softly." Students will develop a feel for dynamic levels by using this activity.

DYNAMIC VOCAL EXERCISES

Use any vocal exercise that is not too difficult for the class. Try the exercise, singing *mf*. This is a middle dynamic range and should be a normal, comfortable tone for students. Sing the exercise three more times using the following dynamic levels in order: *mp, p, pp*. Start the exercise once again at *mf*, and this time work for a louder—but not forced—sound. Use the dynamic markings *f* and *ff*.

Draw a crescendo and decrescendo sign on the board.

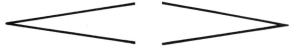

Sing each note of the scale and direct a crescendo and decrescendo as each note is held. It will be necessary to hold each note for a very slow four counts.

Do the following exercise using accents, crescendi and decrescendi. Try it in several different keys.

SONGS ABOUT DYNAMICS

The following songs will help students remember dynamic markings and levels. Each song can be taught individually and should always be sung at the dynamic level which the words suggest. The songs may also be sung one after the other without stopping, because they are all in triple time and in the key of F. Singing the songs one after the other gives the students a comparison of dynamic levels.

Mezzo Forte

Me - di - um loud, Me - di - um loud, sing a mel - o - dy,

Not too loud and not too soft, Just "m - f" if you please.

Forte

For - te, For - te

Loud and ro - bust, Sing "f" this way.

Fortissimo

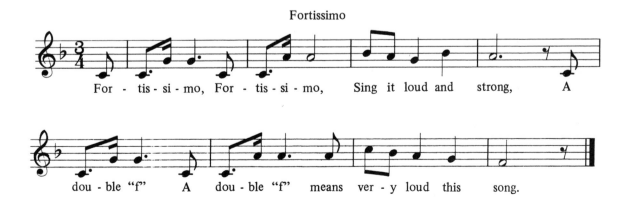

For - tis - si - mo, For - tis - si - mo, Sing it loud and strong, A

dou - ble "f" A dou - ble "f" means ver - y loud this song.

DYNAMIC COLORS

Make copies of the "Dynamic Colors" worksheet and distribute them to students. Students are to follow the key for coloring the pictures.

LOUD OR SOFT?

Make copies of the "Loud or Soft?" worksheet and distribute them to students. This sheet makes students aware of music that is played either loudly or softly.

DYNAMIC WORDSEARCH

Make copies of the "Dynamic Wordsearch" and distribute them to your students. Students are to find names of dynamic markings in the wordsearch.

DYNAMIC COLORS

Color each picture below by using this key:

p = BROWN   pp = YELLOW   ff = PINK   mf = BLUE   mp = BLACK

LOUD OR SOFT?

Look at each of the following types of music. If you think it should be played SOFTLY, put a "p" in front of it. If you think it should be played LOUDLY, put an "f" in front of the type of music.

_____ 1. A marching band in a parade

_____ 2. The prelude played before a religious service

_____ 3. A rock band playing at a concert

_____ 4. A parent singing a lullaby to a baby

_____ 5. Music being played in a restaurant

_____ 6. A teenager with a radio

_____ 7. Music played at a funeral

_____ 8. Music played in the waiting room of a doctor's office

_____ 9. Music played at a high school dance

_____10. A Dixieland jazz band in New Orleans

_____11. A flute playing a solo

_____12. Music played at a political rally

_____13. An opera singer singing an aria

_____14. Bagpipes playing in Scotland

_____15. The recessional at a wedding

_____16. Program music portraying a peaceful day

_____17. Music at a party

_____18. Music played while you're on hold on a telephone

_____19. Music played as background to a speech

_____20. A stereo in a teenager's bedroom

Name _____ Date _____

DYNAMIC WORDSEARCH

Look at the dynamic words at the bottom of this sheet and find each one in the wordsearch below. The words are written either horizontally or vertically.

```
M  E  Z  P  I  A  N  O  B  F  C
F  O  R  T  I  S  S  I  M  O  R
F  A  S  S  R  T  O  E  P  R  C
S  C  Y  D  A  B  F  E  I  T  D
E  C  F  G  M  H  T  I  A  E  L
D  E  C  R  E  S  C  E  N  D  O
Y  N  O  K  Z  L  M  N  I  Z  U
N  T  O  P  Z  S  R  T  S  L  D
A  B  C  D  O  F  G  H  S  I  K
M  L  S  T  H  P  I  E  I  S  P
I  B  R  C  N  S  D  F  M  R  T
C  R  E  S  C  E  N  D  O  I  O
```

PIANO	FORTISSIMO	ACCENT
SOFT	PIANISSIMO	FORTE
LOUD	DECRESCENDO	DYNAMIC
MEZZO	CRESCENDO	

FROSTY FOLK MUSIC: The Bulletin Board

Objective: Students will acquire a knowledge and pride of their heritage by singing folk songs.

Materials Needed:

 Light blue background paper
 Construction paper (dark blue, white, various other colors)
 Cotton
 Tissue paper (various colors)
 Scissors
 Straight pins
 Glue
 Felt-tip markers

Construction Directions:

1. Use an opaque projector or transparency to trace the lettering onto the dark blue construction paper. Attach the letters to the background paper with pins.
2. Draw the staff and song titles onto the background paper with a black felt-tip marker.
3. Trace the snow people onto white paper with a black felt-tip marker. Add facial features.
4. Draw hats and shoes on various colored construction paper and glue these onto the snow people.
5. Use strips of tissue paper for flowing scarves and aprons.
6. Attach the snow people to the background paper using pins.
7. Use construction paper or markers for stick arms.
8. Glue cotton onto the snow people for a fluffy effect.

FROSTY FOLK MUSIC: Unit Activities

This mid-winter snowman theme fits very well into the folk song unit entitled "Frosty Folk Music." The last part of January is often a dreary time, and folk music can liven up the music classroom. Folk music is a part of our national heritage, and it should be included in the curriculum of the music classroom. Often old, familiar folk songs are omitted from current music textbooks, so ten appropriate songs have been included in this unit. Beginning grades may sing only the chorus of a few songs. By adding a few songs at each grade level, older students

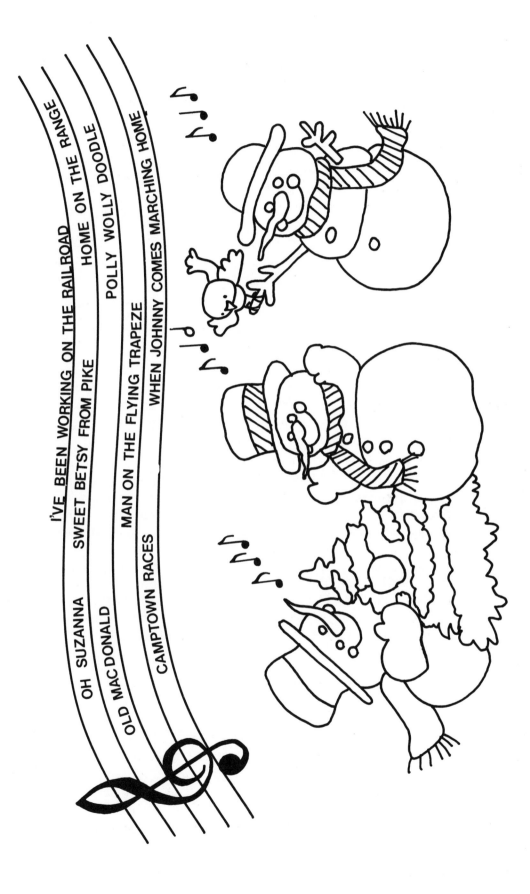

will acquire a full repertoire of folk songs. Let students add names of folk songs to the staff at the top of the board. See how many folk songs can be named by the end of the unit even though not all of them can be sung.

"POP! GOES THE WEASEL"

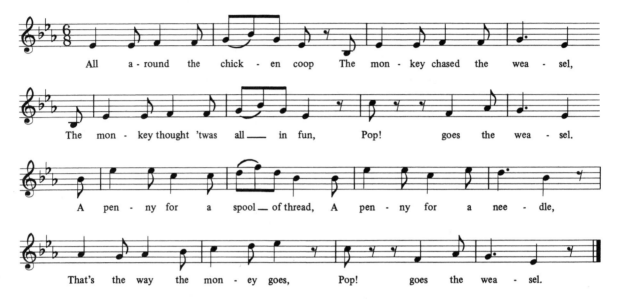

Many people think "Pop Goes the Weasel" is a song about two animals, a monkey and a weasel. Actually, the song is not about animals at all. Long ago in England a "weasel" meant a pressing iron. The monkey was also a part of the machine. The tailor, who worked to make and press clothes, sometimes didn't have enough money to finish buying materials he needed to make the clothes. He would pawn his pressing iron to pay for the materials. "Pop" means to pawn. When he was finished, he would sell the clothes and use the money to buy back his pressing iron. Many of our earliest folk songs came from England along with the early settlers. "London Bridge" is one of the games children probably played as they sailed to America. There are many other folk songs that came from England besides "London Bridge" and "Pop Goes the Weasel."

"BLOW THE MAN DOWN"

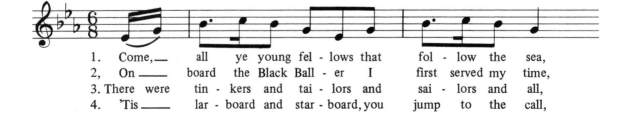

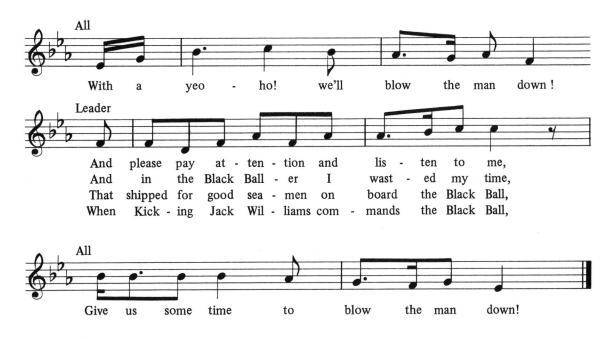

All

With a yeo - ho! we'll blow the man down !

Leader

And please pay at - ten - tion and lis - ten to me,
And in the Black Ball - er I wast - ed my time,
That shipped for good sea - men on board the Black Ball,
When Kick - ing Jack Wil - liams com - mands the Black Ball,

All

Give us some time to blow the man down!

The earliest settlers in North America came by ship. They settled on the east coast, and many continued to earn their living by sailing. The sea songs of these sailors were called *chanties*. The chanties made the hard work of the sailors seem easier. Not only did the songs brighten the men's mood, they supplied the rhythm for their hard tasks such as pulling, lifting, and pushing. When the men needed to work faster, they sang faster. If the winds were strong and carrying the ship with speed the men could relax and sing at a slower tempo.

"SWING LOW, SWEET CHARIOT"

Swing low, sweet char - i - ot,— Com - ing for to car - ry me home!

Fine

Swing— low, sweet char - i - ot,— Com - ing for to car - ry me home.

I looked o - ver Jor - dan, and what did I see?—

"SWING LOW, SWEET CHARIOT" (cont.)

Com - ing for to car - ry me home,

A band of an - gels com - ing af - ter me,

D.C. al Fine

Com - ing for to car - ry me home.

Spirituals are religious songs that often sound "jazzy" because of the syncopation found in the rhythms. Many of them originated on the plantations of the South and are about the trials and troubles and sorrows of this world. The themes of the songs offer hope of a better life to come after death.

"YANKEE DOODLE"

Fa - ther and I went down to camp,
Yan - kee Doo - dle went to town,

A - long with Cap - tain Good - 'in,
a - rid - ing on a po - ny,

And there we saw the men and boys
Stuck a feath - er in his hat

As thick as has - ty pud - din'.
and called it mac - a - ro - ni.

Refrain

Yan - kee Doo - dle, keep it up,

Yan - kee Doo - dle Dan - dy,

"Yankee Doodle" is a Revolutionary War song. The British came with fine uniforms of red, hats with fancy feathers or "macaroni," and guns that matched, and they marched in impressive formations. They arrived and saw the Americans who were often dressed in rags with no hats, had inferior weapons, and no marching order whatsoever. The British laughed at the Americans and called them "Yankee Doodles" or "Silly Englishmen." They began singing a song to taunt the Americans and they even used it to march into battle. (Every troop had a drummer and a fife player, and a song was always used to march into battle.) The British were so confident that they sang "Yankee Doodle" as they marched into battle against the Americans. Much to their surprise, the Americans won the battle. From then on it was the Americans who marched into battle to the tune of "Yankee Doodle". It was as if to say, "How dare you make up a song to ridicule us! We'll show you who the 'Yankee Doodles' really are." The Americans eventually won the war, and "Yankee Doodle" remains a favorite song after all these years.

"SWEET BETSY FROM PIKE"

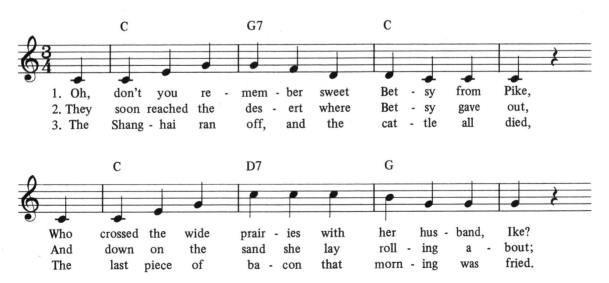

1. Oh, don't you re - mem - ber sweet Bet - sy from Pike,
2. They soon reached the des - ert where Bet - sy gave out,
3. The Shang - hai ran off, and the cat - tle all died,

Who crossed the wide prair - ies with her hus - band, Ike?
And down on the sand she lay roll - ing a - bout;
The last piece of ba - con that morn - ing was fried.

"SWEET BETSY FROM PIKE" (cont.)

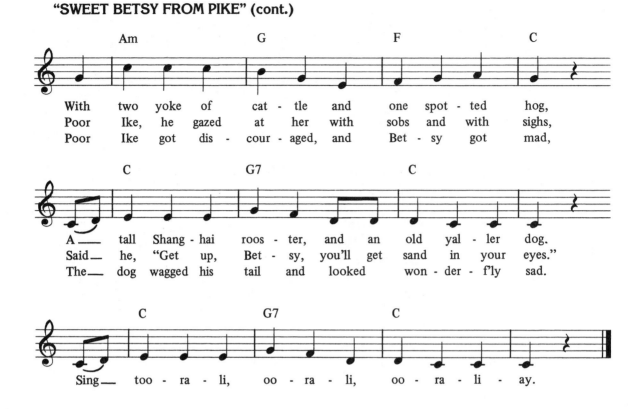

With   two   yoke   of   cat - tle   and   one   spot - ted   hog,
Poor   Ike,   he   gazed   at   her   with   sobs   and   with   sighs,
Poor   Ike   got   dis - cour - aged,   and   Bet - sy   got   mad,

A ___   tall   Shang - hai   roos - ter,   and   an   old   yal - ler   dog.
Said ___   he,   "Get   up,   Bet - sy,   you'll   get   sand   in   your   eyes."
The ___   dog   wagged   his   tail   and   looked   won - der - f'ly   sad.

Sing ___   too - ra - li,   oo - ra - li,   oo - ra - li - ay.

As the east coast became settled, more and more people began moving west to California. They loaded covered wagons with all their belongings and often had to leave much of their furniture and precious keepsakes behind. They faced many hardships as they crossed the prairies, deserts, and mountains. Often they were attacked by Indians, suffered from starvation, died in the deserts, or were caught in mountain blizzards. The trip was not easy, but still people traveled west. They made light of their troubles and hardships by singing songs such as "Sweet Betsy from Pike." There are many more verses than those we provide here, telling of the trials faced by Betsy and Ike as they traveled west.

"DRILL, YE TARRIERS"

1. ___   Ev - 'ry   morn - in'   'round   sev - en   o' - clock,   There   are
2. The ___   boss - 's   name ___   was   Tom ___   Mc - Cann,   And   I'm
3. Next   day   when   pay - day   came ___   a - round,   Tom ___

four and twen - ty men a - drill - in' on the rock, And the
tell - ing ___ you, he's a darn ___ mean ___ man! One ___
Goth ___ a ___ dol - lar ___ short ___ was ___ found, When he

boss comes 'round and he says, "Keep still, And ___
day a pre-ma - ture ___ blast went off, And ___
asked what for ___ Came ___ this re - ply, "You was

bear down heav - y on that old steel drill." ___
up in the air ___ shot ___ old Tom Goth! ___
docked for the time ___ you was up in the sky!" ___

Oh, drill, ye tar - ri - ers, drill. Oh, drill, ye tar - ri - ers, drill! Oh, you

work all day for the sug - ar in your tay, And you stand by your drill,

And you blast a - way, Oh ___ drill, ye tar - ri - ers, drill.

One of the great achievements of the nineteenth century was the railroad, which eventually reached from the east coast to the west coast. It required hard manual labor to blast, tunnel, and lay the tracks. Often Irish laborers, or tarriers, toiled under terrible conditions and mean bosses to accomplish the job. One of the songs they sang as they worked was "Drill, Ye Tarriers." No one really knows why they were called tarriers. Some say it was because their red Irish beards resembled terrier dogs, and others say it is because they dug and tunneled like terriers. The song tells about twenty-four men working on the railroad under their mean boss, Tom McCann. When a premature blast went off, Tom Goth was shot up in the air. The boss was so mean he docked Mr. Goth's pay $1.00 for not working while he was in the air. Although an exaggeration, the song does portray the poor working conditions of the railroad workers who made only enough money to pay for the "sugar in their tay" (tea).

"HOME ON THE RANGE"

Where sel - dom is heard a dis - cour - ag - ing word,

And the skies are not cloud - y all day.——

As the West became settled, the American cowboy emerged. The cowboy led a lonely life on the prairies herding cattle, branding them, and riding the range. His songs often had the rhythm of a jogging horse. Sometimes they were slow and peaceful to quiet the grazing cattle. Long hours in the saddle gave him a great deal of time to sing songs. Later by the campfires at night, singing was a main source of entertainment. Because so much time was spent out of doors, the cowboy actually had a "home on the range."

"DOWN THE RIVER"

1.-3. The riv - er is up, and the chan - nel is deep,

1. The wind is stead - y and strong.—— Oh, won't we have a
2. The wind is stead - y and strong.—— Oh, Di - nah, put the
3. The wind is stead - y and strong.—— The waves do splash from

jol - ly good time, As we go sail - ing a - long.
hoe - cake on, As we go sail - ing a - long.
shore to shore, As we go sail - ing a - long.

Down the riv - er, oh, down the riv - er, Oh,

down the riv - er we go - o - o; Down the riv - er, oh,

slower

down the riv - er, Oh, down the O - hi - o.——

In addition to the railroad, America's rivers were a main source of transportation. Before the railroad, river boats were the only method of transport, and even after the railroad, rivers reached towns and cities that were not connected by the railroad. There were many kinds of boats on the river, including keelboats, flatboats, and later, steamboats. The manual labor required to keep these boats traveling was hard and heavy. Songs such as "Down the River" helped provide rhythms to make the work easier and aided the men to work in unison as a team.

"HOP UP MY LADIES"

The early settlers and pioneers were their own sources of entertainment. Their entertainment was often in the form of music. Meetings were often held where everyone sang, danced, or listened to local musicians. Everyone for miles around would ride their horses, walk, or bring their wagons to attend the event which was simply called a "meeting." This song, "Hop Up, My Ladies," is about attending one of these old fashioned "meetings."

"SKIP TO MY LOU"

2. I'll get another, a better one, too.
3. Can't get a redbird, a bluebird'll do.
4. Cat's in the buttermilk, skip to my Lou.
5. Flies in the sugar bowl, shoo, fly, shoo.

American singing games were played at the "meetings" of the pioneers. Usually the local fiddler, banjo picker, bass player, and guitar strummer would provide the music. The men, women, and children joined together in singing games that later developed into square dancing. "Skip to My Lou" is one of the lively tunes that could be heard in the barns and meeting places of early America. It has countless verses, as do many of the old American folk songs. Many of these verses have been lost over the years.

JANUARY ANSWER KEY

Loud or Soft?

1.	f	11.	p
2.	p	12.	f
3.	f	13.	f
4.	p	14.	f
5.	p	15.	f
6.	f	16.	p
7.	p	17.	f
8.	p	18.	p
9.	f	19.	p
10.	f	20.	f

Dynamic Wordsearch

```
M  E  Z  P  I  A  N  O  B  F  C
F  O  R  T  I  S  S  I  M  O  R
F  A  S  S  R  T  O  E  P  R  C
S  C  Y  D  A  B  F  E  I  T  D
E  C  F  G  M  H  T  I  A  E  L
D  E  C  R  E  S  C  E  N  D  O
Y  N  O  K  Z  L  M  N  I  Z  U
N  T  O  P  Z  S  R  T  S  L  D
A  B  C  D  O  F  G  H  S  I  K
M  L  S  T  H  P  I  E  I  S  P
I  B  R  C  N  S  D  F  M  R  T
C  R  E  S  C  E  N  D  O  I  O
```

February

"Valentine Values"

"Let's 'Ear' It"

VALENTINE VALUES: The Bulletin Board

Objective: Students will increase their knowledge of note values and rhythms.

Materials Needed:

Light pink background paper
Construction paper (red, dark pink, white)
Tissue paper or lace doilies
Scissors
Straight pins
Glue
Black felt-tip marker

Construction Directions:

1. Use an opaque projector or transparency to trace the lettering onto the red construction paper.
2. Trace the hearts using the opaque projector. Use shades of red, white, and dark pink construction paper.
3. Attach the hearts to the background paper with pins.
4. Write in the notes with a black felt-tip marker.
5. Decorate the large heart with crinkled or pleated tissue paper. (NOTE: You might want to use paper doilies instead of tissue paper.)

VALENTINE VALUES: Unit Activities

Rhythms and note values need to be studied in detail at some time during the year. February is a good time to do this, because the values can be shown so clearly on a heart divided into note values. Study sheets beginning with simple color pages and fill-in pages are included in this unit. They are followed by more difficult worksheets for upper-grade students. The students should refer daily to the bulletin board to complete the worksheets. They may want to add circles, squares, rectangles, and other shapes to the board to show note values.

VALENTINE VALUES

Make copies of the "Valentine Values" worksheet and distribute them to students. Students are to color the hearts using the color code.

LABEL THE NOTES

Make copies of the "Label the Notes" sheet and distribute them to students. This activity gives students practice in identifying whole notes, dotted half notes, dotted quarter notes, dotted eighth notes, half notes, quarter notes, eighth notes, and sixteenth notes.

VALENTINE VALUES

NOTE VALUE QUIZ

Make copies of the "Note Value Quiz" sheet and distribute them to students. Students may use the bulletin board to help them find the correct answers.

DRAW THE NOTES

Make copies of the "Draw the Notes" worksheet and distribute them to students. The sheet reinforces their knowledge of notes and meter.

NOTE VALUE PROBLEMS

Make copies of the "Note Value Problems" activity sheet and distribute them to students. The students are to add the note values and solve the problems.

DRAW THE BAR LINES

Make copies of the "Draw the Bar Lines" worksheet and distribute them to students. The activity gives students practice in correctly placing bar lines for the indicated time signatures.

WRITE THE COUNTS

Make copies of the "Write the Counts" sheet and distribute them to students. Students are to write the correct counts under the notes for each measure.

MISSING TIME SIGNATURES

Make copies of the "Missing Time Signatures" worksheet and distribute them to students. This sheet gives students practice in figuring out correct time signatures.

RHYTHM MATCH

Make copies of the "Rhythm Match" worksheet and distribute them to students. This sheet reinforces students' knowledge of symbols and descriptions.

NOTE-COUNT GAME

Make copies of the gameboard and distribute one copy to each group of three to five players. Make a die for each gameboard using a cube of wood with the fol-

The first player rolls the die and moves a playing piece to the appropriate box on the gameboard. The player must correctly name the value of that note. If he or she correctly names it, he or she moves again. If not, then the next player throws the die and moves. Students continue taking turns until one player has reached the end.

VALENTINE VALUES

Color each valentine using this code:

o = BLUE   𝅗𝅥 = YELLOW   ♩ =PINK   = GREEN   ♪ = RED

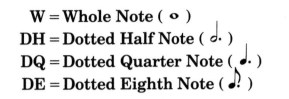

LABEL THE NOTES

Label each note with the proper letter according to this key:

W = Whole Note (○)   H = Half Note (𝅗𝅥)
DH = Dotted Half Note (𝅗𝅥.)   Q = Quarter Note (♩)
DQ = Dotted Quarter Note (♩.)   E = Eighth Note (♪ or ♫)
DE = Dotted Eighth Note (♪.)   S = Sixteenth Note (♬ or ♬)

NOTE VALUE QUIZ

Fill in each blank with the correct number or word. You may look at the "Valentine Values" bulletin board if you need help.

1. Two whole notes equal _____ quarter notes.

2. It takes _____ eighth notes to make one half note.

3. This ♩ is a _____ note.

4. Six eighth notes equal _____ quarter notes.

5. A dot adds _____ of the note's value.

6. One whole note equals _____ eighth notes.

7. It takes _____ sixteenth notes to make one quarter note.

8. Sixteenth notes have _____ flags.

9. One half note equals _____ quarter notes.

10. _____ and _____ notes do not have the heads colored in.

11. It takes _____ eighth notes to equal a whole note.

12. _____ notes have the heads colored in, but no flags.

13. _____ sixteenth notes equal two quarter notes.

14. Eighth notes have _____ flag.

15. A _____ note has the smallest note value of the notes shown on the "Valentine Values" bulletin board.

16. Sixteen sixteenth notes equal _____ whole note(s).

17. It takes _____ quarter notes to equal one whole note.

18. This 𝅝 is a _____ note.

19. A _____ note has the greatest value.

20. This ♪ is a _____ note.

DRAW THE NOTES

Fill in each blank with the correct answer.
(Some questions may have more than one correct answer.)

1. Draw four quarter notes. _____

2. What is needed to make a total of four counts?
   𝅗𝅥 ♩ ♪ _____

3. Draw two quarter notes and two eighth notes.

   _____

4. Draw, in this order, one quarter note, two whole notes, and four sixteenth notes. _____

5. Which note is out of order? ♩ ♩ ♪ ♪ ♪ ♩ 𝅝 𝅝

   _____

6. Draw a dotted half note and four eighth notes. _____

7. What is needed to make three counts? ♩ ♪ ♪ _____

8. Fill in these measures:

   $\frac{3}{4}$ 𝅗𝅥 | ♫. | ♩ | ♫ | ‖

9. Draw, in this order, one whole note, one half note, and two eighth
   notes: _____

10. Which note is out of order? 𝅝 𝅗𝅥. 𝅗𝅥 ♪ 𝅗𝅥. ♩

   _____

11. Draw, in this order, one sixteenth note, two quarter notes, and four
    half notes: _____

12. What is needed to make four counts? ♫ ♫ _____

13. Fill in these measures:

    $\frac{2}{4}$ ♪ ♪ | | ♩ | ♪ | ‖

DRAW THE NOTES cont.

14. Draw, in this order, one whole note and six half notes:

_____

15. Which note is out of order? ♪ ♪ ♩ 𝅗𝅥 ♫ 𝅗𝅥. 𝅝

_____

16. Draw ten sixteenth notes: _____

17. What is needed to make four counts? ♩ _____

18. Fill in these measures:

$\frac{4}{4}$ 𝅗𝅥 | ♩ ♩ ♩ | ♫ ♩ ♫ | 𝅗𝅥. ‖

Name _____ **Date** _____

NOTE VALUE PROBLEMS

Add these note values and solve the problems.

1. 𝅗𝅥 + 𝅗𝅥. = _____

$\frac{?}{4}$

6. ♫ + ♫ + 𝅗𝅥. = _____

2. ♪ + 𝅝 + 𝅗𝅥. = _____

7. 𝅗𝅥 + 𝅗𝅥 + 𝅗𝅥. + 𝅝 = _____

3. ♫ + ♪ + ♪ = _____

8. ♫ + ♫ + ♪ + 𝅗𝅥 = _____

4. 𝅗𝅥. + 𝅗𝅥. + 𝅗𝅥. = _____

9. 𝅗𝅥. + 𝅗𝅥. + ♪ + 𝅗𝅥. = _____

5. ♫ + 𝅘𝅥 + 𝅝 = _____

10. 𝅝 + 𝅗𝅥 + ♪ + ♪ = _____

1. ♪ + ♪ + ♪ = _____

$\frac{?}{8}$

6. ♫ + ♪ + 𝅗𝅥 + 𝅗𝅥. = _____

2. 𝅘𝅥 + 𝅘𝅥 + 𝅘𝅥 = _____

7. ♪ + 𝅗𝅥. + 𝅘𝅥 + 𝅗𝅥 = _____

3. 𝅗𝅥 + 𝅗𝅥 + 𝅗𝅥 = _____

8. ♪ + ♪ + ♪ + 𝅘𝅥 = _____

4. 𝅗𝅥 + ♪ + 𝅗𝅥. = _____

9. 𝅗𝅥 + 𝅗𝅥. + ♪ + 𝅘𝅥 = _____

5. 𝅗𝅥. + 𝅗𝅥 + ♪ = _____

10. 𝅗𝅥 + 𝅗𝅥 + ♪ + ♪ = _____

1. 𝅗𝅥 + 𝅗𝅥 + 𝅗𝅥 = _____

$\frac{?}{2}$

6. 𝅗𝅥 + 𝅘𝅥 + 𝅘𝅥 + 𝅘𝅥 = _____

2. 𝅝 + 𝅗𝅥 + 𝅗𝅥 = _____

7. 𝅝 + 𝅗𝅥 + 𝅝 + 𝅗𝅥 = _____

3. 𝅝 + 𝅘𝅥 + 𝅘𝅥 = _____

8. 𝅘𝅥 + 𝅘𝅥 + 𝅗𝅥 + 𝅝 = _____

4. 𝅘𝅥 + 𝅗𝅥 + 𝅝 = _____

9. 𝅘𝅥 + 𝅘𝅥 + ♫ + 𝅗𝅥 = _____

5. 𝅝 + 𝅝 + 𝅝 = _____

10. ♫ + 𝅘𝅥 + 𝅝 + 𝅝 = _____

DRAW THE BAR LINES

Draw the bar lines in the correct places for the time signatures shown.

1.

2.

3.

4.

5.

6.

7.

8.

9.

10.

© 1990 by Parker Publishing Company

Name_____ Date_____

WRITE THE COUNTS

Look at each time signature and then write the correct counts under the notes.

1. $\frac{3}{4}$

2. $\frac{4}{4}$

3. $\frac{2}{4}$

4. $\frac{6}{8}$

5. $\frac{3}{8}$

6. $\frac{2}{2}$

7. $\frac{4}{4}$

8. $\frac{3}{4}$

9. $\frac{6}{8}$

10. $\frac{4}{4}$

MISSING TIME SIGNATURES

Write the correct time signature at the beginning of each example.

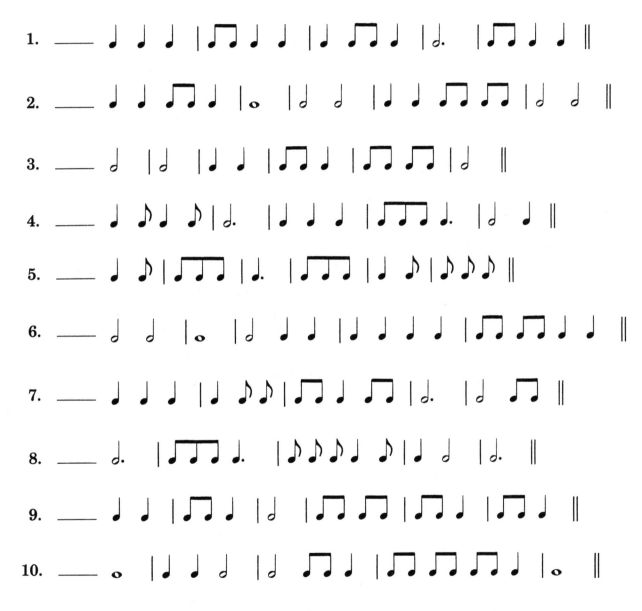

RHYTHM MATCH

Match the symbols on the left to their descriptions on the right.

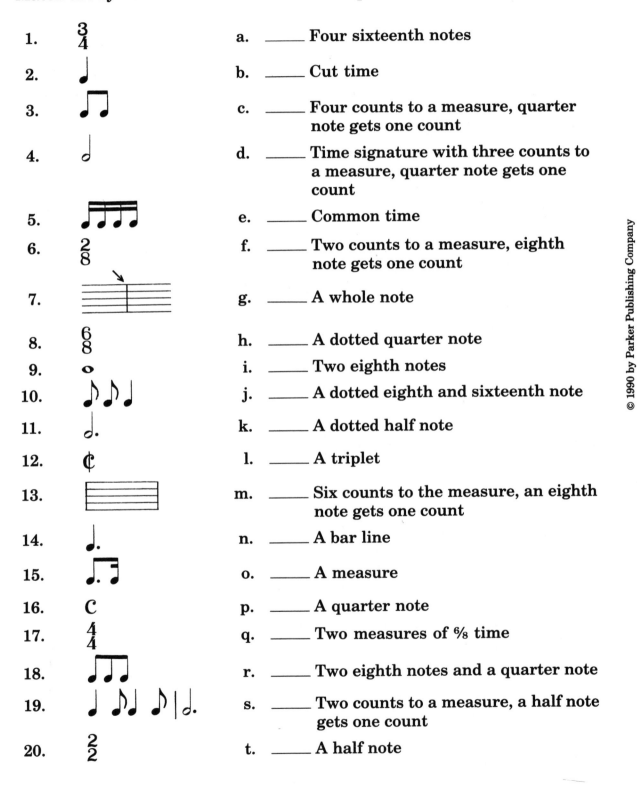

1. $\frac{3}{4}$

2. ♩

3. ♫

4. 𝅗𝅥

5. ♬♬

6. $\frac{2}{8}$

7.

8. $\frac{6}{8}$

9. 𝅝

10. ♪♪♩

11. 𝅗𝅥.

12. ¢

13.

14. ♩.

15. ♩.♪

16. C

17. $\frac{4}{4}$

18. ♫♪

19. ♩ ♪♩ ♪♪|𝅗𝅥.

20. $\frac{2}{2}$

a. _____ Four sixteenth notes

b. _____ Cut time

c. _____ Four counts to a measure, quarter note gets one count

d. _____ Time signature with three counts to a measure, quarter note gets one count

e. _____ Common time

f. _____ Two counts to a measure, eighth note gets one count

g. _____ A whole note

h. _____ A dotted quarter note

i. _____ Two eighth notes

j. _____ A dotted eighth and sixteenth note

k. _____ A dotted half note

l. _____ A triplet

m. _____ Six counts to the measure, an eighth note gets one count

n. _____ A bar line

o. _____ A measure

p. _____ A quarter note

q. _____ Two measures of ⁶⁄₈ time

r. _____ Two eighth notes and a quarter note

s. _____ Two counts to a measure, a half note gets one count

t. _____ A half note

NOTE-COUNT GAMEBOARD

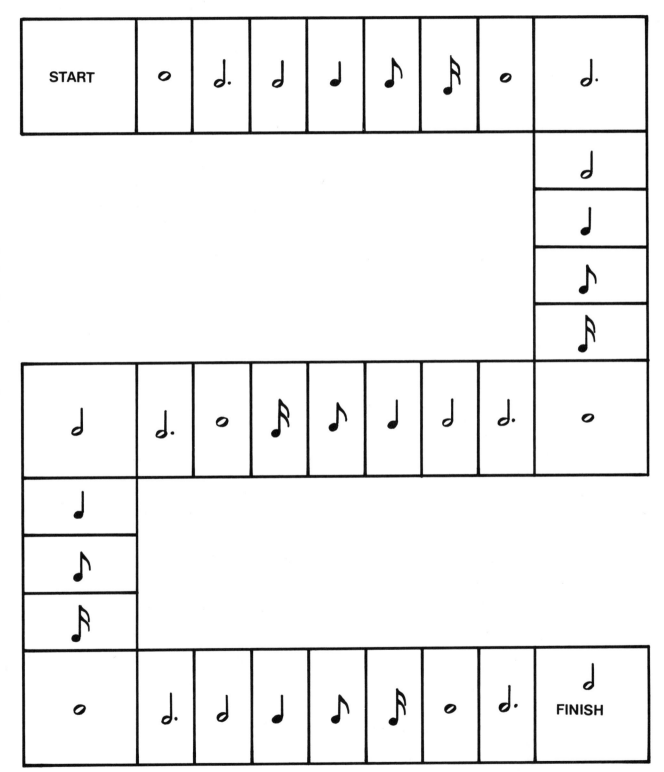

LET'S "EAR" IT: The Bulletin Board

Objective: Students will improve their listening skills by practicing ear training exercises and listening to recordings.

Materials Needed:

Light blue background paper
Construction paper (brown, skin-tone, white, black, pink)
Black yarn
Scissors
Straight pins
Glue
Felt-tip markers

Construction Directions:

1. Use an opaque projector or transparency to trace the lettering onto the black construction paper. Pin the lettering to the light blue background paper.

2. Cut out the large ear from skin-tone construction paper and position it under the word "Ear."

3. Use an opaque projector to trace the characters. Cut out the figures from construction paper. Use white for the rabbit and mouse, grey for the elephant and dog, and skin-tone for the boy.

4. Pin the figures to the background paper. Use pink construction paper for the insides of the animals' ears. Bend or fold all the ears so that they flop out from the board.

5. Make whiskers and hair out of yarn, and glue in place.

6. Use various colors of construction paper for collars.

LET'S "EAR" IT: Unit Activities

This bulletin board emphasizes the sense of hearing. "Let's 'Ear' It" is the theme, and ears of various characters are highlighted. Any type of ears may be used to suggest the listening theme. Students may bring in other characters with interesting ears to add to the bulletin board. Discuss bird's ears or snake's ears, since they can't be seen.

Ear training is an essential part of the music classroom. This should begin with echo clapping in kindergarten and advance to dictation and critical listening of classical music in the upper grades. This unit will begin with simple listening lessons to distinguish same, different, fast, slow, up, down, loud, soft, steps, skips, tone color, etc. Lessons will then advance to listening lessons focusing on melody, harmony, rhythm, tone color, and form.

LET'S "EAR" IT

ECHO CLAPPING

One of the first listening skills to be developed should be echo clapping. This may begin in kindergarten with "my turn, your turn." The teacher claps a rhythm and then students echo the rhythm. Do rhythms one after the other without losing a beat. Start with quarter and eighth notes and gradually advance to harder rhythms at each grade level. (Use many different combinations before progressing to more difficult levels.)

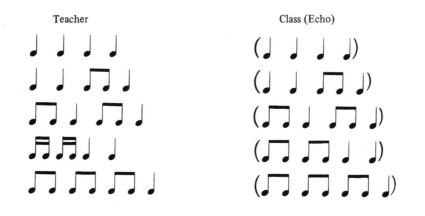

More advanced examples:

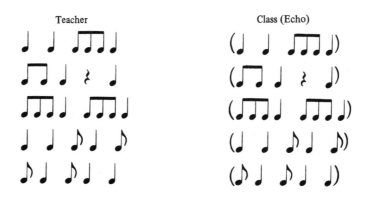

Variations of Echo Clapping

1. Have ten rhythms listed on the board. Ask, "Which one did I clap?"
2. Let students clap rhythms and lead the exercise.
3. Do echo clapping with students one beat behind the teacher. (They are listening to one rhythm and clapping another.)

EITHER-OR

Play many examples of "Either-Or" for the class. One day it may be "Same or Different." There are numerous suggestions for playing this game given in "Flower Forms" (May). Another day the teacher may choose to play examples of "Fast or Slow." (See suggestions given in March's "Tempo Trail.") Students may call out the answers, or you may give five to ten quick written ear training exercises at the beginning of class. It is a good idea to alternate ear training with sight-reading because of lack of time.

Another category of listening exercises could be "Up or Down"—play two short melodies that go up or down and see if students can identify them. After students can identify ascending and descending melodies, play melodies in steps or skips. Students should be able to verbalize "going up in steps" or "going down in skips."

Study tone color and test students' skills in identifying various musical instruments on recordings. (See November's "Missing Mystery Instrument" for additional suggestions.)

DICTATION

The ability to take musical dictation depends upon the amount of time spent learning the skill. This, as well as sight-reading, playing skills, and so on, must be presented in steady, sequential lessons. A small amount of time must be spent each week in development of listening skills. It is impossible to teach these skills in one unit each year. Ear training is a cumulative process, with each step built upon the previous one. The skills must be constantly used in order to progress to the subsequent steps. Start in kindergarten with "Echo Clapping." Next, have students go to the chalkboard and take simple dictation of quarter and eighth notes. Gradually progress to more difficult rhythms and rests. The proper sequence is explained in November's "Turkey Tunes." Take simple sight-reading rhythms and use them for dictation. After students are able to take rhythmic dictation, advance to melodic dictation.

GUIDED LISTENING

Sometimes it is helpful to have a general listening sheet that could be used for any listening lesson. Students may simply answer the questions on the "Guided Listening Sheet," or use the questions as a guide for writing a paper or discussing the music.

LISTENING QUIZ

For each of the five examples listed on the "Listening Quiz" are questions for older students to answer as they listen. You may want to select separate questions when guiding younger students in listening. Younger students may not be able to grasp every concept, so it may take several days to cover the material. Older students may need several class sessions to listen to an example and answer the questions. Use the "Listening Quiz" as a model for making additional quizzes for listening lessons.

GUIDED LISTENING SHEET

Keep these questions in mind as you listen to the music.

1. TEMPO:
   - Is it slow?
   - Is it fast?

2. DYNAMICS:
   - Is it soft?
   - Is it loud?

3. HARMONY:
   - Can you hear the harmony?
   - Is it major or minor?

4. MOOD:
   - Is it happy?
   - Is it sad?

5. MELODY:
   - What instruments play the melody?
   - Is the melody high or low?

6. FORM:
   - Do you hear any sections repeated?

7. RHYTHM:
   - Is it smooth and flowing?
   - Is it hard and driving?

8. TIMBRE:
   - What instruments do you hear?

LISTENING QUIZ

Appalachian Spring, "Simple Gifts"

1. The composer of *Appalachian Spring* is:
   a. Beethoven   b. Copland   c. Mozart
2. The introduction is played by:
   a. strings   b. brass   c. woodwinds
3. The main theme is played by:
   a. strings   b. brass   c. woodwinds
4. The first solo instrument to play is:
   a. clarinet   b. trumpet   c. violin
5. The second solo instrument to play is:
   a. clarinet   b. oboe   c. flute
6. Variation 4 is played by:
   a. strings   b. brass   c. woodwinds
7. Variation 4 is:
   a. loud   b. soft
8. The form of this music is:
   a. symphony   b. suite   c. theme and variation
9. The introduction starts:
   a. softly   b. loudly
10. A theme is a:
    a. composition   b. main melody   c. variation

Little Fugue in G Minor

1. The music begins with:
   a. the subject   b. the answer   c. the episode
2. The music was originally composed for:
   a. orchestra   b. harpsichord   c. organ.
3. A fugue is most like a:
   a. pop song   b. round   c. symphony
4. The music:
   a. stops in places   b. continues in motion
5. The music becomes:
   a. softer   b. louder

6. A fugue is:
   a. monophonic   b. homophonic   c. polyphonic
7. The composer of this piece is:
   a. Bach   b. Beethoven   c. Mozart
8. The texture:
   a. starts thin and becomes thick   b. starts thick and becomes thin
9. The instruments are mainly:
   a. strings/woodwinds   b. strings/brass   c. percussion/brass
10. The last chord is:
    a. major   b. minor

Water Music Suite, "Hornpipe"

1. The composer is:
   a. Haydn   b. Handel   c. Mozart
2. The form of this music is:
   a. theme and variations   b. suite   c. symphony
3. A suite is:
   a. a theme with various melodies   b. a round
   c. a set of dances
4. *Water Music Suite* was written for:
   a. King George I   b. Queen Elizabeth II
   c. George Washington
5. The music was first played on:
   a. a barge   b. an airplane   c. the radio
6. It is called *Water Music Suite* because:
   a. it was first played while floating down the river
   b. it sounds like the running of a river
   c. it was played to make rain
7. The melody is first played by:
   a. trumpets/clarinets   b. oboes   c. violins
8. The first melody is answered by:
   a. oboes   b. clarinets   c. violins
9. The music is:
   a. exciting   b. stately   c. jazzy

LISTENING QUIZ cont.

10. The meter of the music is:
    a. duple   b. triple

"Hoedown"

1. The composer is
   a. Bartók   b. Debussy   c. Copland
2. The form of the music is:
   a. ABA   b. ABAC   c. ABCD
3. Does the song have an introduction and coda?
   a. Yes   b. No
4. The mood of the piece is:
   a. sad   b. happy
5. This music is from a:
   a. ballet   b. suite   c. symphony
6. The music is based on:
   a. a hymn   b. music from the West   c. a ballad
7. The rhythm is:
   a. syncopated   b. not syncopated
   c. always on the beat in triple meter
8. The rhythms are accented by use of:
   a. violins   b. piano   c. percussion instruments
9. A hoedown is a:
   a. dance   b. funeral   c. wedding
10. The music ends:
    a. softly   b. loudly

Variations on "Pop Goes the Weasel"

1. The introduction is played by:
   a. percussion instruments   b. woodwind instruments
   c. whole orchestra
2. The theme is played by:
   a. clarinets   b. the orchestra   c. percussion
3. The first variation is a:
   a. fugue   b. march   c. waltz

LISTENING QUIZ cont.

4. The second variation is in:
   a. duple meter   b. triple meter

5. Variation 3 is played by:
   a. trumpet   b. bassoon   c. violin

6. Variation 3 sounds:
   a. happy   b. sad

7. How many variations are there?
   a. one   b. four   c. five

8. Which drum announces that something is about to happen?
   a. bass   b. snare   c. kettle

9. After the slow section comes a variation that sounds like a:
   a. march   b. funeral song   c. music box

10. The composition ends with a:
    a. flute   b. trumpet   c. saxophone

FEBRUARY ANSWER KEY

Label the Notes

1. Q, W, E, DH, S, H, DQ
2. DE, S, DH, Q, W, E, DH
3. DQ, E, W, S, DE, DH, Q
4. W, Q, E, S, DH, E, S
5. H, DQ, DE, W, Q, E, S
6. DH, E, S, H, DQ, DE, W

Note Value Quiz

1. 8
2. 4
3. quarter
4. 3
5. ½
6. 8
7. 4
8. 2
9. 2
10. whole and half

11. 8
12. quarter
13. 8
14. 1
15. sixteenth
16. 1
17. 4
18. whole
19. whole
20. sixteenth

Draw the Notes

1.
2. Answers will vary.
3.
4.
5.
6.
7. Answers will vary.
8. Answers will vary.
9.

10.
11.
12. Answers will vary.
13. Answers will vary.
14.
15.
16.
17. Answers will vary
18. Answers will vary.

Note Value Problems

?/4

1.	5	6.	5
2.	7½	7.	10
3.	2	8.	4
4.	6	9.	8
5.	5½	10.	7

?/8

1.	3	6.	12
2.	6	7.	10
3.	12	8.	4
4.	8	9.	13
5.	11	10.	10

?/2

1.	3	6.	2½
2.	4	7.	6
3.	3	8.	4
4.	3½	9.	2½
5.	6	10.	5

Draw the Bar Lines

7. 𝄴 (rhythm notation)

8. 𝄵 (rhythm notation)

9. 𝄵 (rhythm notation)

10. 𝄴 (rhythm notation)

Write the Counts

1. 3/4 (rhythm notation)
12 3 1 2 3 1 + 2 3 1 + 2 + 3 + 123

2. 4/4 (rhythm notation)
1234 12 34 1 + 2 3 + 4 123 4 12 3 + 4

3. 2/4 (rhythm notation)
12 1 2 1 + 2 + 1 + 2 1 2 12

4. 6/8 (rhythm notation)
12 3 45 6 1 2 3 4 5 6 123456 123456 1 2 3 456

5. 3/8 (rhythm notation)
12 3 12 3 1 2 3 123 12 3 1 2 3

6. 2/2 (rhythm notation)
1 2 12 1 2 + 1 2 1 + 2 + 12

7. 4/4 (rhythm notation)
12 34 1234 1 2 3 + 4 1 + 2 + 3 4 + 12 3 + 4

8. 3/4 (rhythm notation)
12 3 1 + 2 + 3 + 1 2 3 1 + 2 3 + 1 + 23

9. 6/8 (rhythm notation)
1 2 3 456 12 34 56 123456 1234 56 1 2 3 45 6

10. 4/4 (rhythm notation)
12 34 1 2 3 4 1 + 2 3 + 4 + 123 4 1234

Missing Time Signatures

1. $\frac{3}{4}$ 6. $\frac{4}{4}$

2. $\frac{4}{4}$ 7. $\frac{3}{4}$

3. $\frac{2}{4}$ 8. $\frac{6}{8}$

4. $\frac{6}{8}$ 9. $\frac{2}{4}$

5. $\frac{3}{8}$ 10. $\frac{4}{4}$

Rhythm Match

a.	5	k.	11
b.	12	l.	18
c.	17	m.	8
d.	1	n.	7
e.	16	o.	13
f.	6	p.	2
g.	9	q.	19
h.	14	r.	10
i.	3	s.	20
j.	15	t.	4

Listening Quiz

Appalachian Spring, "Simple Gifts"

1.	b	6.	b
2.	a	7.	a
3.	c	8.	c
4.	a	9.	a
5.	b	10.	b

Little Fugue in G Minor

1. a   6. c
2. c   7. a
3. b   8. a
4. b   9. a
5. b   10. a

Water Music Suite,"Hornpipe"

1. b   6. a
2. b   7. c
3. c   8. a
4. a   9. b
5. a   10. b

"Hoedown"

1. c   6. b
2. a   7. a
3. a   8. c
4. b   9. a
5. a   10. b

Variations on "Pop Goes the Weasel"

1. c   6. b
2. b   7. c
3. a   8. b
4. b   9. c
5. c   10. a

March

"Learning Notes with the Lazy Leprechaun"

"The Tempo Trail"

LEARNING NOTES WITH THE LAZY LEPRECHAUN:
The Bulletin Board

Objective: Students will learn note names by filling in worksheets, playing games, and playing instruments.

Materials Needed:

    Light green background paper
    Construction paper (black, dark green, skin-tone, tan, white)
    Yarn (black or grey)
    Scissors
    Straight pins
    Glue
    Felt-tip marker

Construction Directions:

1. Use an opaque projector or transparency to trace the letters onto black construction paper. Attach the letters to the board with pins.
2. Trace the leprechaun, shamrocks, and grass onto dark green construction paper.
3. Trace the mushroom onto tan construction paper. Trace the leprechaun's face and hands onto skin-tone construction paper.
4. Cut out the figures and attach to the background with pins.
5. Use yarn for the strings and the leprechaun's beard.
6. Use a felt-tip marker to write the staves and notes on white paper. Attach these to the shamrocks.

LEARNING NOTES WITH THE LAZY LEPRECHAUN:
Unit Activities

Learning note names is a vital part of the music program. Students need exercises and games to encourage them in their knowledge of reading music. They should also have practice playing instruments to use this knowledge. Usually elementary students work with only the treble clef, and worksheets provided in this unit are for treble clef only. The teacher may use the examples to make additional worksheets using bass clef for advanced groups or upper grades. Change the notes on the shamrocks daily, and ask students to name the notes. This could be a daily "warm-up" activity for the month of March.

LINE OR SPACE

Before students can read music from the staff, they must be able to tell whether the notes are on the lines or spaces of the staff. This may be so elemen-

LEARNING NOTES WITH THE
LAZY LEPRECHAUN

tary that many teachers skip this step altogether. But, students who have music-reading problems often are having trouble with this fundamental concept. Draw a staff on the board and put whole notes on the various lines and spaces of the staff. Tell students, "When a note is on a line, the line of the staff runs through the middle of the note. When the note sits between two lines of the staff it is on a space." Point to various notes and have students call out "line" or "space."

After students are able to identify whole notes as "line" or "space" notes, try other notes—which are harder to identify—with stems and flags. Still work from the board so all students can observe.

Line or Space Worksheet

Hand out a worksheet with notes on a staff for students to identify. They should mark the line notes "L" and the space notes "S." Here are some examples to help you get started:

NAMING NOTES

Note names may be taught by using mnemonics, such as "Every Good Boy Does Fine," for the line notes, or "F-A-C-E" for the spaces. The teacher may also show the first line is "E" and have students figure alphabetically (E,F,G,A,B,C,D,E,F). The mnemonic method may be faster, but the alphabetical concept will make learning notes on the bass clef and notes on ledger lines easier. Whichever method is used, work from the board first, so all students can see and learn together. Draw a staff with notes on the board and lead students in figuring out note names.

There are only nine notes, so draw them and ask each student to name a note. When finished with the staff, start over so every student names a note. The next music class, hand out a sheet with notes on a staff. Review on the chalkboard, then do the worksheet together. Most students aren't ready to try the worksheet on their own yet. The next time the class meets, hand out another worksheet with notes and let students attempt naming them by themselves. Only use one staff of notes on this first worksheet. Have students bring papers to your desk to be checked. As soon as one student has named all notes correctly, assign that student to help another student who may be having difficulty. The next worksheet may be longer, but students can still help each other. Finally, give a test to confirm that the concept has been mastered.

DRAW THE NOTE

In this activity, instead of having students name the note, students draw the note on the proper line or space. When notes can be drawn two places on the staff (F and E), use both places. Use the same procedure as when learning the note names.

1. Draw a staff with letters under it on the board and have students come forward to draw the note on the proper line or space.
2. Review and hand out a worksheet where students must draw the note on the proper line or space. Work together with the class.
3. Hand out a short worksheet and check as students finish. Have students who finish correctly help students having trouble.
4. Hand out a longer work sheet and let students help each other.
5. Test.

NOTE NAME FLASH CARDS

Naming notes requires a great deal of practice before students are able to recognize the notes quickly enough to play them on an instrument. Drill with flash cards is an excellent way to master the skill. Flash cards can be purchased in local music stores, through catalogs, or the teacher can make several sets of flash cards so students can practice by themselves. It is best to work in couples with one person naming notes and the other showing the notes. If working with limited sets of flash cards, the teacher could divide the class into three or four groups. One person in each group could show the cards and the rest of the group guesses the name of the note. If only one set of flash cards is available, the teacher may show the cards while students name notes together.

NOTE TOSS

Using masking tape, put a large staff on the floor. Students use a plastic coffee can lid, butter dish lid, etc. to throw on the staff. As the lid lands on various lines and spaces of the staff, students receive points if they can name the note. The person with the most points at the end of the game is the winner.

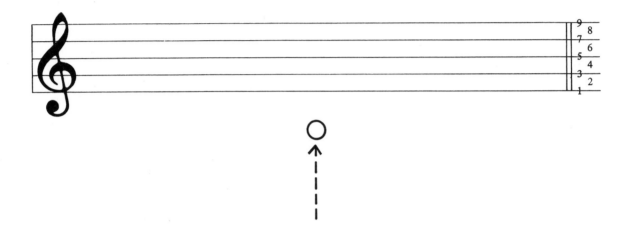

PLAYING INSTRUMENTS

It is difficult for students to play instruments in the music classroom because there are usually not enough instruments to go around or enough time to practice so students can master the skill. A good way to begin with very young students is with "If You're Happy and You Know It, (Play the *C*)." Have students play C on their instruments at the appropriate place in the song. It is possible to change the C to any other note, but as the note changes the key of the song must be changed also.

IF YOU'RE HAPPY

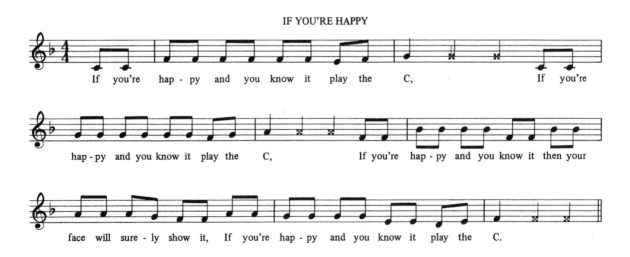

After finding the notes and playing with "If You're Happy and You Know It," students are ready to move to more difficult songs. Even first graders can master all of "Hot Cross Buns."

HOT CROSS BUNS

Hot cross buns, Hot cross bu ns, one a pen - ny, two a pen - ny, Hot cross buns.

Another simple song that is easy for students to play on instruments is "Little Robin Redbreast."

LITTLE ROBIN REDBREAST

Lit - tle Rob - in Red - breast Came to vis - it me.

This is what he whis - tled, "Thank you for my tea."

Students will feel successful even if they can master only one phrase of familiar songs. Encourage them to read the music, play, and memorize the following songs or phrases of the songs. Use simple song material from their music text books also.

"Twinkle Twinkle Little Star"
"This Old Man"
"Jingle Bells"
"Mary Had a Little Lamb"
"Jolly Old Saint Nicholas"

SIGHT-READING WITH NOTE NAMES

Students can practice reading notes by transferring syllables or numbers to note names. Follow the examples outlined in November's "Turkey Tunes" and use note names instead of numbers or syllables to read the music. Also, take simple phrases from song material for practice in singing and reading note names.

NOTE NAMES AND SONG MATERIAL

Always use song material to study note names. Ask questions like the following ones to guide students in reading note names.

1. What note does the song start on?
2. What is the name of the last note on the third staff?
3. How many *E*s are on the second staff?
4. How many times is the note repeated at the beginning of the song?
5. How many times do you find the pattern "F,F,E,D,C?"
6. How many *A*s are on the first staff?
7. Read and sing the first five notes of the song.
8. Who can go to the bells or piano and play the first phrase?
9. Go to the board and write the note names of the first staff.
10. Write an introduction or coda to the song and play it.

NOTE NAME COLOR SHEET

Make copies of the "Note Name Color Sheet" and distribute them to your students. Students are to color the shamrocks according to the color key given.

NOTE NAME STORY

Make copies of the "Note Name Story" and distribute them to students. Students are to complete the story by reading the notes representing the missing words.

NOTE NAME COLOR SHEET

Use the following key to color the shamrocks:

NOTE NAME STORY

Can you read this story? Good luck!

Eagle Wing was an Indian boy who wanted more than anything else to be able to hunt with his [♪notes] Brave Fox. He watched his father lead all the braves out of camp on the big hunt, while his mother said, "Now don't be [♪notes] . Go to [♪notes] and take a nap. Your [♪notes] will be home soon." Instead of sleeping in the tepee, Eagle Wing smeared red, yellow, and blue paint on his [♪notes] , put on his special [♪notes] necklace, and picked up his [♪notes] of arrows. He sneaked under the back [♪notes] of the tepee and ran to his horse, Paint. Paint and Eagle Wing raced to the hill where the braves were already killing buffalo. Many buffalo were [♪notes] , and his [♪notes] was off his horse ready to skin the big bull he had killed. Suddenly the bull jumped up and Eagle Wing raced toward his [♪notes] . He reached in his [♪notes] of arrows and aimed quickly. As soon as the arrow struck, the big bull fell only inches from his father. Brave Fox looked at his son and smiled. "Tonight we will have a celebration," he said. "We will [♪notes] on buffalo [♪notes] , corn, and [♪notes] . It will be a feast to honor you, Eagle Wing. You have done a brave [♪notes] , and from now on you will hunt with the men."

THE TEMPO TRAIL: The Bulletin Board

Objective: Students will learn various tempo markings by associating them with animals, by singing tempo songs, and by using a metronome.

Materials Needed:

Light green background paper
Construction paper (dark green, brown)
Brown yarn
Feathers
Black felt-tip marker
Glue
Scissors
Straight pins

Construction Directions:

1. Draw the trail on the background with a black marker.
2. Use an opaque projector or transparency to trace the lettering onto black construction paper. Attach the cut-out letters to the background with pins.
3. Trace the rocks and animals onto brown construction paper.
4. Use dark green construction paper for the grass. Pin to the background paper and fold blades of grass out for a three-dimensional effect.
5. Cut out the figures and attach them to the board with pins.
6. Decorate the bird with colored feathers.
7. Decorate the coyote with yarn.
8. Decorate the turtle shell with green construction paper.
9. Use a black felt-tip marker to write the words under the animals.

THE TEMPO TRAIL: Unit Activities

Use your imagination in creating the "Tempo Trail." Any kind of path through a wooded area can be used. Along this path are various animals suggesting slow, medium, and fast speeds. Animals will help students relate to and remember the tempo names. Although presto, moderato, and andante are used here, students should find other tempo markings and suggest animals that would be appropriate.

Have students go to the bulletin board and choose a tempo marking to pin to the board. Sing any familiar song to that tempo. Have a different student put up

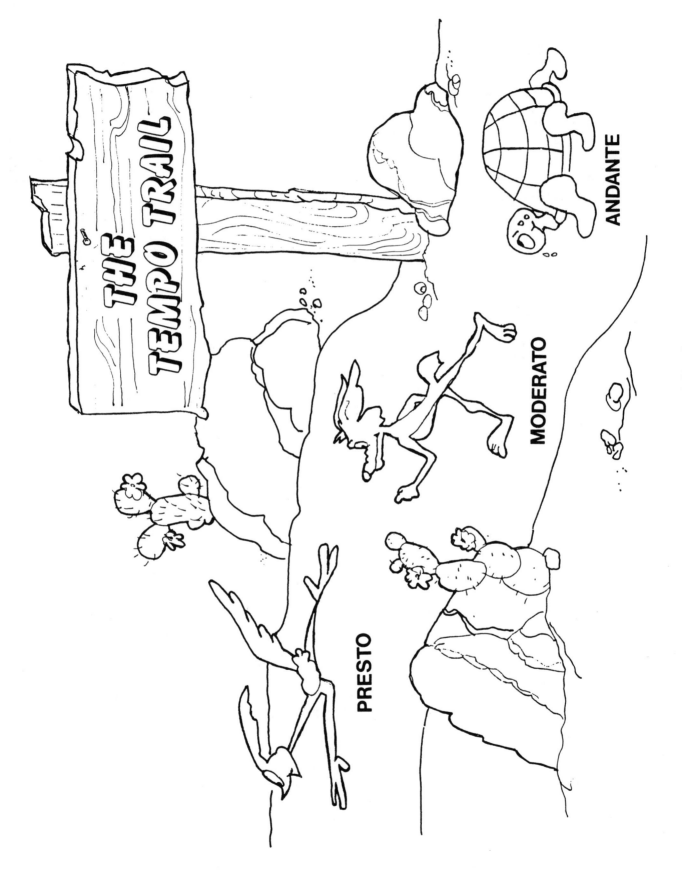

a different tempo marking. Sing the same song to that tempo. Each day sing a song to various tempo markings using this procedure.

TEMPO ANIMALS

Introduce the words from the bulletin board, *presto, moderato,* and *andante.* Explain to the students that these are Italian words, because printed music began in Italy and we still use Italian terms today. Ask students to guess what the words mean by how the animals are moving. Tell the students speed in music is called "tempo," and that is why the bulletin board is called "Tempo Trails." Discuss other animals that could represent fast, medium, and slow. Have students make posters, drawing three different animals representing presto, moderato, and andante. The posters will be displayed on the wall or board to help students remember the tempo markings.

FASTER, SLOWER

Clap two rhythms that are identical, but in different tempos. Have students say whether the second example is faster or slower than the first example. After students have had experience as a class, pass out a worksheet. The sheet should be numbered one through ten with "faster" and "slower" printed next to each number. Students are to circle the correct answer as each example is clapped by you. You may want to play the examples on an instrument if you prefer. Each set of rhythms should be clapped or played identically, except for the tempo.

LISTENING AND LABELING TEMPOS

In every listening example, students should classify the tempo of the music. Many pieces get faster or slower during the composition. Even young students can identify faster or slower parts of the music. Older students should be introduced to the words *accelerando* and *ritardando*. Play listening examples for students to identify accelerandi and ritardandi. Give them many opportunities to listen to changes of tempo in recorded music.

MOVING TO TEMPO

Young students should have many experiences moving to music. After students are able to march to music played on the piano, change the tempo of the music. This activity will not work with recorded music because you cannot change the tempo of the music. Play the music faster—stop—more slowly—stop—original speed—stop—faster—etc. After students have mastered the skill, don't stop between changes and see if students can adjust from one tempo to the next. When students have mastered marching music, change to sliding, skipping, or running. (See the examples given in October's "Movin' and Groovin'.")

PERFORMING TEMPO

Choose simple songs that students know well. Each song should have several verses. Start the song slowly, and with each verse speed up the tempo. Students enjoy this activity and it allows them to perform in various tempos. Be careful that students don't get louder with each verse. The volume should remain the same—only the tempo should change. Some songs that could be used for this activity are "Skip to My Lou," "Old MacDonald," "He's Got the Whole World in His Hands," "She'll Be Coming Round the Mountain," "Mary Had a Little Lamb," "Yankee Doodle," and "This Old Man."

NOTATING TEMPO

Choose a familiar song and copy the words on the board. Let the class write tempo markings throughout the song. Sing the song with tempo markings supplied by students. Change tempo markings and sing the song again. After changing the markings several times, decide which tempo markings fit the song best. Perform the song a final time.

USING THE METRONOME

The metronome is an invaluable aid in teaching tempo. Set the dial or slide to various numbers and let students say whether the tempo is faster or slower. Try singing familiar songs to different tempo settings, and see if students can stay with the metronome. Use familiar songs and sing them at a "normal" tempo. Let students decide which tempo setting the metronome should use to match the tempo.

SHEET MUSIC AND TEMPO

Sheet music that is in parts is more likely to have tempo markings than music found in the students' texts. Pass out copies of a song and discuss tempo markings found in the song. Discuss the metronome setting number at the beginning of the song. Use a metronome to demonstrate designated tempos. To test students, pass out additional sheet music and let students list tempo markings.

SONGS FOR TEMPO

Sing the songs (on the next page) about tempo to help students remember tempo markings.

TEMPO WORDSEARCH

Make copies of the "Tempo Wordsearch" and distribute copies to your students. Students are to find tempo related words in the wordsearch.

Andante

An - dan - te, An - dan - te, slow, slow, slow, _____

Like a tur - tle, Creep a - long, _____ slow, slow, _____ slow.

Moderato

Not too fast and not too slow, ____ Mod - er - a - to, here we go.

Nice and stead - y, Keep it flow - ing, Mod - er - a - to.

Presto

Hur - ry, scur - ry, race a - long, Rush - ing, rush - ing, through the song,

Pres - to, pres - to, don't be slow, Pres - to's fast, oh, don't you kn ow?

Hur - ry, scur - ry, race a - long, Rush - ing, rush - ing, through the song,

Pres - to, pres - to, tem - po can't be slow.

TEMPO WORDSEARCH

Look at the tempo words at the bottom of this sheet and find each one in the wordsearch below. The words can be found either horizontally or vertically.

```
L  R  A  L  L  E  G  R  E  T  T  O
A  A  C  C  E  L  L  I  A  E  P  M
R  A  C  C  E  N  A  T  D  M  R  E
P  R  E  S  T  O  R  A  A  P  E  T
A  L  L  A  L  L  G  R  G  O  S  R
L  C  E  F  E  R  O  D  A  M  A  O
F  E  R  M  A  T  A  A  D  A  G  N
A  N  A  N  D  A  N  T  E  R  D  O
R  A  N  A  L  L  E  G  R  O  N  M
D  O  D  R  A  D  A  G  I  O  T  E
E  M  O  A  C  C  E  N  T  P  O  R
```

ACCELERANDO	ACCENT	ADAGIO
ALLEGRETTO	LARGO	ALLEGRO
PRESTO	ANDANTE	TEMPO
FERMATA	METRONOME	

MARCH ANSWER KEY

Note Name Story

1.	DAD	9.	DEAD
2.	BAD	10.	DAD
3.	BED	11.	DAD
4.	DAD	12.	BAG
5.	FACE	13.	FEED
6.	BEADED	14.	BEEF
7.	BAG	15.	CABBAGE
8.	EDGE	16.	DEED

Tempo Wordsearch

```
L R (A L L E G R E (T) T O)
A A (C C E L (L) I A E P M
R A  C C E N A T D M R E
(P R E S T O) R A A P E T
A L  L A L L G R G O S R
L C  E F E R O D A M A O
(F E R M A T A) A D A G N
A N (A N D A N T E) R D O
R A N (A L L E G R O) N M
D O D R (A D A G I O) T E
E M O (A C C E N T) P O R
```

April

"Showers of Scales"

"Rainbow of Rests"

SHOWERS OF SCALES: The Bulletin Board

Objective: Students will increase their understanding of scales by playing and constructing scales.

Materials Needed:

Dark blue background paper
Construction paper (light blue, yellow, black, white)
Scissors
Straight pins
Glue
Black felt-tip pen

Construction Directions:

1.   Use an opaque projector or transparency to trace the letters onto white construction paper. Attach the letters to the board with pins.
2.   Trace the raindrops and puddle onto light blue construction paper.
3.   Use either black paper letters or a felt-tip marker for the lettering on the puddle.
4.   Trace the umbrella and lower handle onto yellow construction paper. Use a black felt-tip marker to outline the handle.
5.   Attach all figures to the background paper.
6.   Use a black marker to write the scale letters onto the raindrops.

SHOWERS OF SCALES: Unit Activities

This bulletin board consists of the familiar "April Showers" theme. These showers are raindrops of scales, half steps, whole steps, etc. It is a simple bulletin board to construct, appropriate for the season and it displays an important learning concept for students. Because scales and chords are the basis of all music, students should understand how they're used in composition. Even very young students can play a "C" scale or a pentatonic scale and then advance to other more complicated scales. Students will recognize the sound of a scale and they are very pleased with themselves when they can play simple scales. They will be able to play these scales before they will understand the structure using whole steps and half steps. Scales will be studied on a very elementary level and then advance to a more complete study of the structure of scales. Each day choose students to play scales from the bulletin board raindrops. If students master all the scales shown, put new scales on the raindrops and have them play the new scales.

SONGS OF SCALES

The following songs for the major, pentatonic, and chromatic scales will help students learn and then remember the scales.

SCALE PERFORMANCE

A scale center can be set up in the hall just outside the music classroom door. If bells and rubber mallets are used it will be quiet enough not to bother other classrooms. Begin with the C major scale. After students have been shown the scale, send them outside the room one at a time to play the scale. It is possible to have a piano student stay outside the room to help those having problems. If bells are limited, this is a good way to assure everyone gets to play the scale. As the regular lesson continues in the music classroom, students leave the room one at a time to play the scale. As one returns, the next student goes to the scale center. Begin with the C scale and continue on other days to the F, G, pentatonic, chromatic and any other scales.

PENTATONIC ACCOMPANIMENT

Learn the song "Angel Band."

ANGEL BAND

Use bells or Orff instruments to construct accompaniment patterns for the song. Because any pattern will fit with a pentatonic accompaniment, students may have freedom to choose their own pattern or the following accompaniment patterns may be used. Use other pentatonic melodies and create accompaniments to use with them.

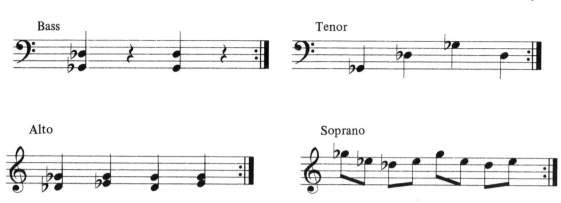

HEAR THE SCALE

After students have had several opportunities to hear and play scales, you may test their ability to identify scales by listening. Make worksheets or tests short, using only five to ten examples. Begin with only major and minor scales. Give students clues for identification, such as bright/happy for major, and sad/dark for minor. Play five to ten major or minor scales in mixed order. Play each scale several times. Students should number their papers and answer either "major" or "minor." When students are successful at distinguishing between major and minor, add chromatic scales. When students can identify major, minor, and chromatic, add pentatonic scales (Oriental sound). Finally, add twelve-tone scales (atonal, modern sound).

After students are able to identify all scales on a worksheet, have them identify the underlying scales for songs you play. It will help to number each example and have students circle the correct answer, such as major, minor, chromatic, pentatonic, or twelve-tone.

FINDING SCALES

As in all learning experiences, students need to apply skills to the music they are singing and playing. Use the music textbook and look for examples of scales in songs that students are singing. Perhaps the entire scale will not be notated in the music, but fragments of scales may be found. For example:

"She'll Be Coming 'Round the Mountain" (beginning is pentatonic)

"All Night, All Day" (B section is pentatonic)

"Twinkle, Twinkle Little Star" (B section is partial major scale backwards)

"Joy to the World" (beginning is major scale backwards)

"This Old Man" ("Give a dog a bone" is major)

"Hey, Ho, Nobody Home" ("merry" is minor)

"Ghost of Tom" (ending is minor)

"Supercalifragilisticexpialidocious" (ending is chromatic)

SHARPS AND FLATS

To deal with whole steps, half steps, and construction of scales students must have a knowledge of sharps and flats (black notes). Supply each student with a set of bells or a diagram of the keyboard. Explain that a sharp raises a note or causes it to go up a half step. A flat lowers it or brings it down a half step. Have students put their finger on G, and give the following instructions: "Now find G♯. It goes up one half step, so your finger should be here." (Demonstrate.) "Put fingers on G again. Now find G♭." Walk around the room to check whether students have their fingers on the correct note. Repeat the process with A and D. Proceed to C and C♯. Students will have difficulty finding C♭. Help them realize when C is lowered by a half step, it is a white note, not a black note. Work with F, E, and B. You may demonstrate all sharps and flats to the class on a diagram on the board or a set of bells. As the next step, students can try finding the notes on a diagram at their seats, and finally, they should try to play them on the bells, xylophone, piano, or other keyboard instrument.

HALF STEPS AND WHOLE STEPS

Hold up a set of bells for the class to see. Explain that a half step is two connected notes—nothing is between them. Demonstrate various half steps to the class. Define a whole step as two notes having one step in between them. Demonstrate various possibilities. Now hold up the bells and put two fingers either a whole step or half step apart. Let students call out which it is. Show several examples. During the next class session review whole and half steps, and then hand out paper and pencils. Students must write "W" for whole step and "H" for half step. For another class activity use diagrams of keyboards. Practice finding whole and half steps up or down from given starting notes. Examples:

"Find G. Put your finger a half step up from G. What is the name of the note?" (G♯)

"Find C. Put your finger one whole step up from C. What is the name of the note?" (D)

"Find A. Put your finger a half step down from A. What is the note?" (A♭)

"Find F. Put your finger a half step down from F. What is the note?" (E)

Walk around the room to see if students are able to find the correct notes.

STUDY OF ANCIENT AND MODAL SCALES

Play an example of Gregorian chant. Encourage students to discuss the example and lead them to the conclusion that one reason the music sounds strange to our ears is that Gregorian chant was based on ancient scales called modal scales. Have a student come forward and play:

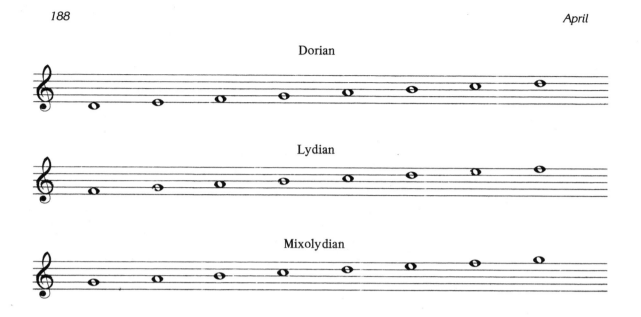

Dorian

Lydian

Mixolydian

BUILDING SCALES

After students are familiar with sharps and flats and whole steps and half steps, they are ready to begin construction of scales using formulas. Discuss the formula of whole and half steps for a major scale.

W   W   H   W   W   W   H

Write the notes of the C major scale:

C   D   E   F   G   A   B   C

When students check the C major scale against the formula they will find that the scale is correct. Explain that when the notes are not correct, it is necessary to either sharp or flat the notes to make the scale fit the formula. Write the notes of the F major scale on the board:

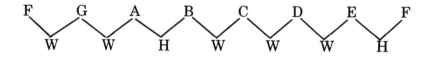

As the teacher helps students check the formula they will find that A to B is a whole step and it should be a half step. Students should change the B to B♭.

Write the G scale:

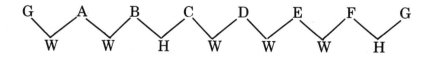

By checking the notes against the formula, you find that F must be changed to F♯ to complete the G major scale.

On different days write various scales on the board and check them against the formula, adding sharps and flats as necessary. It is possible to write the scales as letters on the board or as notes on the staff. If bells are available, have students play each scale.

BUILDING CHORDS FROM SCALES

Introduce the I, IV, and V chords for accompaniment. They will be easy to find when students can build scales from the formula of whole and half steps. Examples:

```
C D E F G A B C       F G A B♭ C D E F       D E F♯ G A B C♯ D
I    IV V             I    IV V              I    IV V
```

To find the notes of the major chords, skip every other note of the scale for the first, fourth, and fifth notes of the scale. Write the notes under the root of the chord.

C Major

I			IV	V				
C	D	E	F	G	A	B	C	(D)
E			A	B				
G			C	D				

D Major

I			IV	V				
D	E	F♯	G	A	B	C♯	D	(E)
F♯			B	C♯				
A			D	E				

Try constructing all the major scales and finding all the chords by using this method. It will take several weeks to complete this activity.

TONE ROWS

Explain that in the early twentieth century, composers became tired of the same instruments, methods, and scales. They were looking for something new. Arnold Schoenberg took the chromatic scale and mixed it up to make new scales called tone rows. Demonstrate tone rows by using resonator bells that can be removed and held individually. Use twelve students with twelve bells in the order of the chromatic scale. Have the students mix up. Play the bells in this mixed-up order, which is a new scale. This new scale is called a tone row. Mix students up several times for several different tone row scales. Explain some of the rules of tone row composition:

1. All notes must be sounded in order.
2. Notes can be sounded forwards.
3. Notes can be sounded backwards.
4. More than one note may be sounded at a time.
5. Inversions and mirror progressions may be used.

Use a tone row as described above, with twelve students each holding a bell. Write a composition following the rules above. Each student sounds his or her bell at the proper time. An example of a twelve-tone composition may be as follows:

Twelve-Tone Composition

1. Form a tone row
2. Play all bells one at a time forwards—from left to right
3. Play all bells one at a time backwards—from right to left
4. Play bells two at a time forwards (4 counts each)
5. Play bells two at a time backwards (4 counts each)
6. Play first six bells together (8 times)
7. Play second six bells together (8 times)
8. Play all bells together (8 times)

RAINBOW OF RESTS: The Bulletin Board

Objective: Students will learn rest values by filling in worksheets and performing rhythms using rests.

Materials Needed:

Dark blue background paper
Construction paper (pastel colors)
Scissors
Straight pins
Glue
Black felt-tip marker

Construction Directions:

1. Use an opaque projector or transparency to trace the lettering onto pastel colored construction paper. Attach the cut-out letters onto the background paper with pins.
2. Trace the rainbow onto various pastel colored papers. As the bulletin board will be large, use large rolls of pastel colored paper if available.
3. Attach the rainbow to the background paper with pins.
4. Use a black felt-tip marker to draw the rests onto the rainbow.

RAINBOW OF RESTS: Unit Activities

This bulletin board continues the theme of "April Showers." The rainbow is a colorful display and a very appropriate way to portray rest values. This unit will serve as a review of the February "Valentine Values" lessons. It will also further students' knowledge of note values by advancing to the study of rests. Students must understand rest values as well as note values to be able to play, sing, and read music. Many of the games and activities used in "Valentine Values" can be used again by substituting rests. The lessons presented in this unit will be more difficult than those presented in February. Because rests are silences, examples and compositions will include combinations of note values and rests. Students should refer to the bulletin board daily to help them complete the worksheets and activities in this unit.

RHYTHMS AND RESTS FLASH CARDS

Flash cards have been used several times already in earlier lessons. Because drill is often so important to the learning process, they are an invaluable aid.

RAINBOW OF RESTS

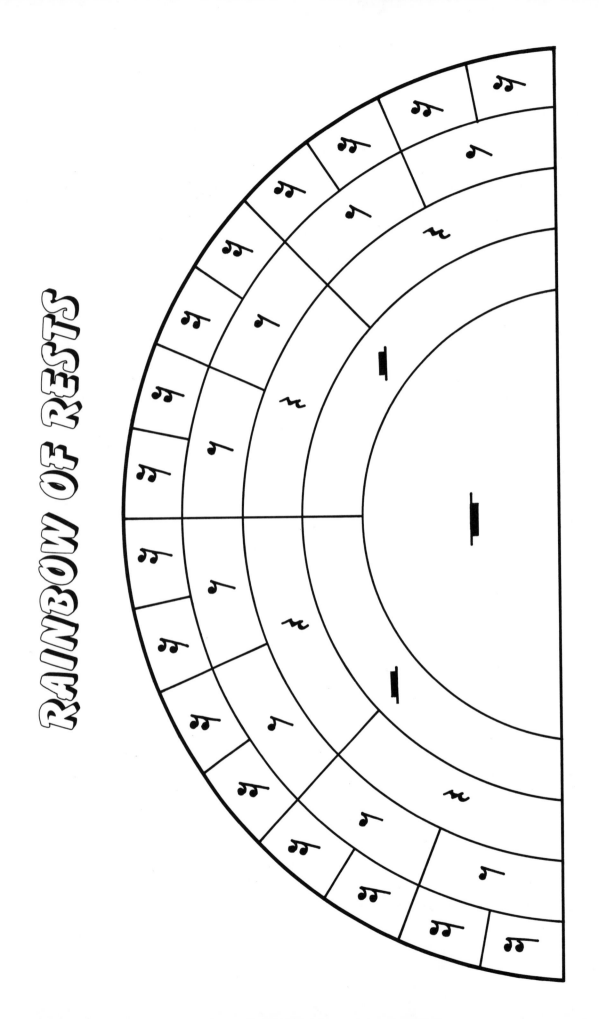

Flash cards made to drill notes and rests should begin with simple quarter notes and rests. Proceed next to eighth notes, then half notes and rests, then whole notes and rests, etc. The following examples give several illustrations of rhythms to display on flash cards in varying degrees of difficulty. You may make up different examples in addition to the ones presented here. Try handing out rhythm instruments and letting students play the flash cards instead of clapping the rhythms.

Quarters

Quarter and Eighth

Half, Quarter and Eighth

Whole, Half, Quarter and Eighth

Advanced Rhythms

FIND THE RESTS

All students should be directed back toward the song material being used in class. It is important that students don't just pick up bits and pieces of isolated information. They must relate this information to reading music. In all printed songs being sung, point out rests. Ask questions like the following:

1. How many rests are on staff 2?
2. What kind of a rest is on staff 1?
3. Can you clap the last staff, using the rests properly?
4. How many counts does the third rest on staff 1 get?
5. Why do we have rests in songs?

RHYTHM BAND

As an extracurricular activity, form a rhythm band for a PTA program or for a class presentation. Students may write their own compositions or use selections from rhythm band books. Work with the group, polish the performance, and present it in a special program. You could have older students perform for younger students. This will give students an opportunity to use the knowledge they have acquired and will help develop playing skills and a sense of achievement.

REST COLOR PAGE

Make copies of the "Rest Color Page" and distribute copies to students. Students are to color the springtime drawings using the key given.

EQUAL VALUES

Make copies of the "Equal Values" worksheet and distribute copies to students. Encourage the students to use the bulletin board to help them answer the value problems.

DRAWING NOTES AND RESTS

Make copies of the "Drawing Notes and Rests" worksheet and distribute them to students. This sheet gives students practice in drawing notes and rests.

ADDITION OF RESTS

Make copies of the "Addition of Rests" activity sheet and distribute them to students. This sheet reinforces students' knowledge of the values of notes and rests.

WRITE THE COUNTS

Make copies of the "Write the Counts" worksheet and distribute them to students. Students are to write the correct counts under the notes in each measure.

FILL IN THE RESTS

Make copies of the "Fill in the Rests" worksheet and distribute them to students. This activity sheet gives students practice in filling in proper counts.

REST COLOR PAGE

Use the codes below to color these pictures.

= Brown   = Yellow   = Orange

= Red   = Green

Name _____ Date _____

EQUAL VALUES

Fill in the following problems. You may refer to the bulletin board for help if necessary.

1. 1 𝅝 = _____ 𝅘𝅥𝅯

16. 2 𝄾 = _____ 𝄽

2. 1 𝄾 = _____ 𝅘𝅥𝅯

17. 1 𝄽 = _____ 𝅘𝅥𝅯

3. 1 𝅗𝅥 = _____ 𝅘𝅥𝅯

18. 2 𝅗𝅥 = _____ 𝅘𝅥𝅯

4. 2 𝄽 = _____ 𝄾

19. 8 𝄾 = _____ 𝅝

5. 8 𝅘𝅥𝅯 = _____ 𝄽

20. 16 𝅘𝅥𝅯 = _____ 𝅝

6. 1 𝅗𝅥 = _____ 𝄾

21. 2 𝅗𝅥 = _____ 𝄽

7. 8 𝅘𝅥𝅯 = _____ 𝅝

22. 2 𝄽 = _____ 𝅝

8. 1 𝅗𝅥 = _____ 𝄾

23. 2 𝄽 = _____ 𝅘𝅥𝅯

9. 2 𝅘𝅥𝅯 = _____ 𝄾

24. 1 𝅗𝅥 = _____ 𝄽

10. 3 𝄽 = _____ 𝅘𝅥𝅯

25. 4 𝄽 = _____ 𝅝

11. 12 𝅘𝅥𝅯 = _____ 𝄽

26. 4 𝄽 = _____ 𝄾

12. 6 𝄾 = _____ 𝅘𝅥𝅯

27. 1 𝅗𝅥 = _____ 𝅗𝅥

13. 16 𝄾 = _____ 𝅝

28. 4 𝅘𝅥𝅯 = _____ 𝄽

14. 1 𝅗𝅥 = _____ 𝄽

29. 2 𝅗𝅥 = _____ 𝄾

15. 4 𝅘𝅥𝅯 = _____ 𝄾

30. 2 𝅗𝅥 = _____ 𝅝

DRAWING NOTES AND RESTS

1. 1 quarter note, 3 eighth rests, 1 whole note   _____

2. 2 whole notes, 5 sixteenth rests, 2 quarter rests   _____

3. 1 half note, 1 eighth note, 2 whole rests   _____

4. 4 quarter notes, 2 eighth notes, 1 quarter rest   _____

5. 3 eighth notes, 1 sixteenth rest, 4 half rests   _____

6. 4 sixteenth notes, 2 eighth notes, 2 sixteenth
   rests   _____

7. 2 whole rests, 1 eighth rest, 4 sixteenth notes   _____

8. 4 half rests, 1 sixteenth rest, 4 quarter notes   _____

9. 3 quarter rests, 2 sixteenth rests, 4 half rests   _____

10. 1 eighth rest, 4 quarter notes, 2 whole notes   _____

11. 5 sixteenth rests, 2 whole rests, 1 eighth note   _____

12. 2 whole notes, 2 half rests, 6 eighth rests   _____

13. 2 half notes, 1 quarter note, 3 sixteenth rests   _____

14. 3 quarter notes, 4 eighth notes, 2 half rests   _____

15. 6 eighth notes, 2 sixteenth rests, 1 whole rest   _____

16. 4 sixteenth notes, 4 eighth notes, 4 quarter rests   _____

17. 2 whole rests, 1 half rest, 4 quarter notes   _____

18. 4 half rests, 2 quarter rests, 4 sixteenth notes   _____

19. 2 quarter rests, 3 eighth rests, 4 half notes   _____

20. 1 sixteenth rest, 4 half rests, 4 sixteenth notes   _____

Name _____ Date _____

ADDITION OF RESTS

Use the following chart of note values to add these "equations." Numbers 1 through 10 use only rests; 11 through 20 use both notes and rests.

= ¼   = ½   = 1   = 2   = 4

1. ♪ + ♪ ♪ + ♪ = ____

2. ♪ + ♪ + ▬ + ▬ = ____

3. ♪ + ♪ + ▬ + ♪ = ____

4. ▬ + ▬ + ▬ = ____

5. ♪ + ♪ + ♪ + ♪ + ▬ = ____

6. ♪ + ▬ + ♪ + ♪ = ____

7. ♪ + ♪ + ♪ + ♪ + ▬ = ____

8. ▬ + ♪ + ♪ + ♪ + ♪ = ____

9. ▬ + ♪ + ▬ + ♪ + ♪ = ____

10. ♪ + ♪ + ♪ + ♪ = ____

11. ♪ + ♪ + o + ▬ = ____

12. ♩ + o + ♪ + ♪ + ♩ = ____

13. ♩ + ♪ + ▬ + ▬ = ____

14. ♩ + ♪ + ♪ + ♪ = ____

15. o + ♪ + ♪ + ♪ = ____

16. ♪ + ♪ + ♪ + ♪ + ♪ = ____

17. ♪ + ♪ + ♪ + ▬ = ____

18. ▬ + ♩ + ♩ + o = ____

19. ♪ + ♪ + ♩ + ♪ = ____

20. ♩ + ♩ + o + ▬ = ____

WRITE THE COUNTS

Write the correct counts under the notes in each measure below. Both notes and rests are used.

BONUS PROBLEMS: The following five are harder. GOOD LUCK!

FILL IN THE RESTS

Fill in each measure with rests to complete the measures.

APRIL ANSWER KEY

Equal Values

1.	16	11.	3	21.	4
2.	2	12.	12	22.	1
3.	8	13.	2	23.	8
4.	4	14.	4	24.	2
5.	2	15.	2	25.	1
6.	8	16.	1	26.	8
7.	1	17.	4	27.	2
8.	4	18.	16	28.	1
9.	1	19.	2	29.	8
10.	12	20.	2	30.	1

Drawing Notes and Rests

© 1990 by Parker Publishing Company

Addition of Rests

1.	2	11.	7
2.	7	12.	7 ½
3.	6 ¼	13.	7 ½
4.	10	14.	3
5.	5	15.	6 ½
6.	6 ½	16.	2 ¾
7.	6	17.	5
8.	5½	18.	9
9.	5	19.	3½
10.	1½	20.	9

Write the Counts

13. (music notation)

14. (music notation)

15. (music notation)

Fill in the Rests

Answers may vary. Here are some suggestions:

1. (music notation)

2. (music notation)

3. (music notation)

4. (music notation)

5. (music notation)

6. (music notation)

7. (music notation)

8. (music notation)

9. (music notation)

10. (music notation)

May

"Flower Forms"

"Composing with Haiku"

FLOWER FORMS: The Bulletin Board

Objective: Students will improve their knowledge of form by studying "same" and "different"; they will label forms of songs that are sung as well as label forms of songs in listening lessons.

Materials Needed:

Light green background paper
Construction paper (black, dark green, bright "flowery" colors)
Tissue paper (optional)
Silk flowers (optional)
Plastic flowers (optional)
Scissors
Straight pins
Glue
Black felt-tip marker

Construction Directions:

1. Use an opaque projector or transparency to trace the lettering onto the black construction paper. Attach the cut-out letters with pins.

2. Cut stems from dark green construction paper and pin them onto the background paper.

3. Trace flower shapes from different colored construction paper. Attach them to the stems with pins. (NOTE: You might want to make flowers from tissue paper or use plastic or silk flowers for an even more attractive bulletin board.)

FLOWER FORMS: Unit Activities

This bulletin board can be very colorful and artistic. Many kinds of flowers and several different materials can be used for the best possible effect. Silk flowers could even be pinned to the board. The sequence of flowers shows form very clearly. Transfer should be made from flower forms (daisy/rose/daisy) to the use of letters (ABA) to show form. Have flowers available to pin on the bulletin board. When singing a song or listening to a song, have students pin flowers to the board to match the song's form. Make this a daily activity when introducing new song material.

DRAW AND COLOR FLOWER FORMS

Tell your students that they are going to draw and color flowers for different forms, such as *aba, abca, abba, abcd*. Write the forms on the chalkboard and have the students use paper and crayons for their drawings. Students should have dis-

FLOWER FORMS

cussed the bulletin board and have had practice in identifying and drawing flowers to indicate form before they try this activity. Encourage students to be creative and use different flowers than those on the bulletin board.

SAME AND DIFFERENT

Form is a relationship of "same" and "different." Students should learn to make comparisons through sight as well as hearing. Without these skills, they will be unable to recognize form. Practice using the following suggestions to distinguish "same" and "different." Students should verbalize or have a worksheet. Use five examples for each suggestion and let students decide if they are the same or different.

1. Clap two rhythms.
2. Play two phrases on the piano.
3. Play two different rhythm instruments that students cannot see.
4. Play two rhythms on the drums.
5. Have two people hiding. One person will say a phrase twice, or both people will say the same phrase.
6. Play two recorded sounds, such as sticks hitting, water running, whistling, a door slamming, or a dog barking.
7. Have students look at two pictures and decide if they are the same or different.
8. Show four shapes and ask the students to tell which shape does not belong.
9. Write a page of rhythms and ask the students to decide whether they are the same or different. For example:

10. Print two fragments of music on staffs. Students must identify them as either the same or different. For example:

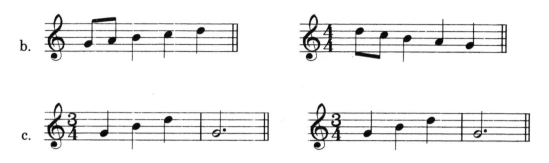

PICK A FLOWER

Have sixteen flowers made of silk or plastic sitting on a desk or table. There should be four flowers each of four designs. As a fragment, line, or phrase of a song is played, various students come forward and choose a flower to fit the form. The "A" person may choose any flower each time. The second person chooses a flower to fit the form and stands next to the first person. Four people will be used for each song and they should stand in line holding the correct flower to show the form of the song. Use simple songs to begin and advance to harder ones, for example, "Hot Cross Buns" *(aaba),* "Twinkle, Twinkle Little Star" *(aba),* "Skip to My Lou" *(abac),* "This Old Man" *(abcd),* and "Pawpaw Patch" *(abac).*

FORM WITH LETTERS

At the next class session after "Pick a Flower," give a test using the same songs, wherein students write out the form of the song after each title. Additional familiar songs may also be used, such as "Old MacDonald" *(aaba),* "John Brown" *(abac),* "Row, Row, Row Your Boat" *(abcd),* "Are You Sleeping?" *(abcd),* and "Kookaburra" *(abcd).*

BEGINNING AND ADVANCING FORM

As each new song is learned, you should lead students in discovering parts that are alike and different, and identifying the form of the song. You might introduce songs taught by rote to young students by saying, "I'm going to sing a new song. Listen and tell me how many times you hear 'Here We Go 'Round the Mulberry Bush.'" With this kind of questioning, students become aware of "same" and "different" in music before they're aware of form. Later, as students are using their music textbooks, ask such questions as "Which two lines of the music are alike?" Make sure students look at the notes of the staff and not the words of the song. Finally, guide older students in determining the form of the song. Ask the following questions:

1. What letter will we name the first phrase of the song? *(a)*
2. Is the second line the same as the first line? If it is, name it *a.* If not, name it *b.* Is the second line *a* or *b*?

3. Look at the third phrase of the song. If it is like the first line, name it *a*. If it is like the second line of the song, name it *b*. If it is different from both the first and second lines, name it *c*.

4. Continue with each line or phrase in the same fashion.

PENTATONIC COMPOSING WITH FORM

Have four different students make up a phrase of pentatonic music using the bells. It is convenient to use pentatonic phrases because they hang together and will sound as if they fit when played one after the other. The first student will be *a*; the second student, *b*; the third student, *c*; and the fourth student, *d*. Each student must remember his or her phrase and be able to play it where required. To begin this activity, write a form on the chalkboard. Start with *abcd,* so that each of the four students will get to play. Have them line up and play the complete song. Then try other forms (*aaba, abca, abacada,* etc.). Although this method requires only that each student create one phrase, many complete songs can be organized from these four phrases.

RHYTHM COMPOSITIONS IN FORM

Once older students are able to fill in measures with the proper number of counts, they are ready to begin composing rhythm compositions using form. For example, use four measures for each phrase and make each phrase in 4/4 time.

```
A    |          |          |          ||
B    |          |          |          ||
C    |          |          |          ||
D    |          |          |          ||
```

After students have filled in the measures with rhythms for each letter, ask students to arrange their rhythmic compositions in various forms. For example:

```
A    |          |          |          ||
B    |          |          |          ||
A    |          |          |          ||
A    |          |          |          ||
B    |          |          |          ||
C    |          |          |          ||
A    |          |          |          ||
```

COMPOSING WITH FORM ON THE STAFF

Hand students a paper with three staffs labeled *aba*. Students must have had many previous experiences of working with rhythms and compositions before they are ready to proceed with notated compositions. Instruct students to fill in the measures with notes using 4/4 time. The first and last lines *must* be alike, and the middle line will be different. Ask students to have their compositions end on C. The teacher may play the compositions when they're finished. Students love to hear their works performed. Because most students will not have experience in composition, these early works will probably not sound too good. Ending on C helps establish a tonality, since sharps and flats are not used. It is also nice if the teacher can add chords that are suggested by the melody line as the compositions are played.

FORM SEARCH

Ask students to find various forms in their song book texts. This is a difficult task, and it can be simplified by suggesting two pages and asking which is the correct page. A worksheet can be organized as follows:

abac: Page 27 Page 94
abcd: Page 32 Page 65
aaba: Page 76 Page 2
aabb: Page 21 Page 110

Look up both pages listed in your book. Circle the correct page number for the form suggested. (The teacher should complete the worksheet using pages in the students' music text books.)

FORM REPORTS

Older students should make reports on various forms. These may be written or oral reports. Some suggested topics are:

Rondo
Sonata Allegro
Suite
Opera
Through-Composed
Symphony
Madrigal
Twelve-Tone Composition
Variation

MATCH THE FORM

Make copies of the "Match the Form" activity sheet and distribute them to students. This worksheet reinforces the students' knowledge of identifying correct form.

MATCH THE FORM

Circle the correct form for each set below.

1. [flower images] = ABCA   ABBA   ABAA

2. [flower images] = ABCA   AABA   ABCD

3. [flower images] = ABCA   ABAB   AABA

4. [flower images] = ABCD   ABCA   ABAB

5. [shape images] = ABCD   ABAB   AABA

6. [shape images] = ABCA   ABAA   AABA

7. [face images] = ABBA   ABAB   ABCA

8. [flower images] = AABA   ABAA   ABCA

9. [shape images] = ABAB   ABAA   AAAB

10. [face images] = AABB   ABAB   AAAA

COMPOSING WITH HAIKU: The Bulletin Board

Objective: Students will improve their knowledge and skills of composition by writing a Haiku poem and setting it to music.

Materials Needed:

Light yellow background paper
Construction paper (black, red, tan)
Patterned wallpaper, cloth, or foil
Scissors
Straight pins
Glue
Black felt-tip marker

Construction Directions:

1. Use an opaque projector or transparency to trace the letters onto black construction paper. Attach the cut-out letters to the background paper with pins.
2. Pleat red paper for the fans.
3. Trace the table on black construction paper; trace the cup and tea pot on red paper, and cut out. Attach to background paper with pins.
4. Trace the clothes onto patterned wallpaper, cloth, or foil, and cut out.
5. Trace the faces, hands, and feet on tan construction paper.
6. Place all figures onto the background paper with pins. Use a black marker to outline the blanket.
7. Students will be writing Haiku during this unit, so display their poems on the folded fans. Change the poems daily so that everyone's Haiku is displayed.

COMPOSING WITH HAIKU: Unit Activities

The man and woman drinking tea in this bulletin board suggest an oriental setting. This is a good time to study pentatonic scales, oriental music, and the culture of Asia. The fans, which also suggest the oriental theme, should display students' best efforts at composing Haiku poetry. The teacher may choose three of the best, or display all poems changing the display each day.

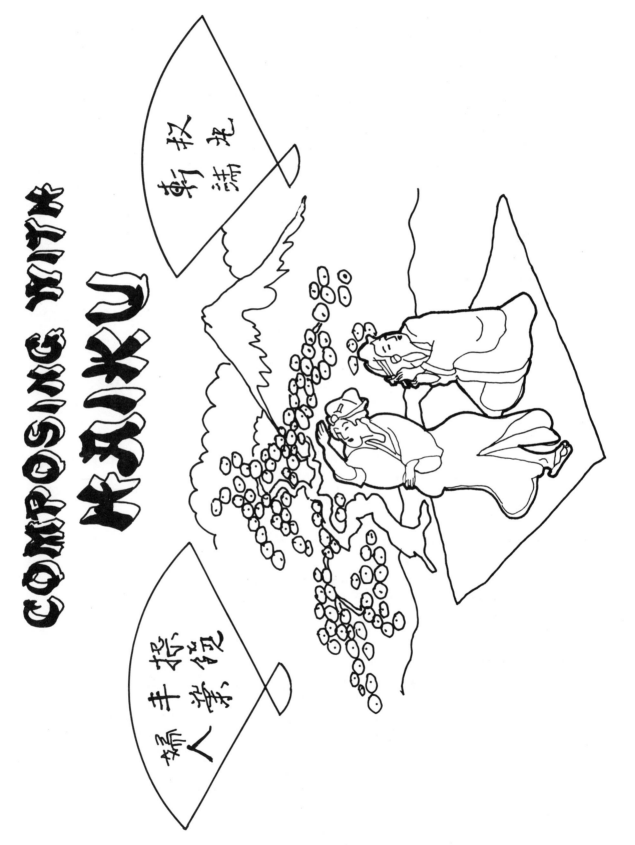

COMPOSING WITH HAIKU

Often lessons on composition are hard to teach. Using Haiku poetry makes this task easier, because it gives a definite form and rules to follow. Also, there are no complete sentences or rhyming in Haiku, only description. Haiku poetry is a short verse form that originated in Japan. Haiku actually means "game-verse." It is a very old form of poetry that dates back to the fifteenth and sixteenth centuries. Americans first became interested in Haiku after World War II, when it became popular in the United States.

Haiku has a total of seventeen syllables. They are arranged in a three line verse of five, seven, and five syllables. Because of its brevity, Haiku has a simple construction. In this simplicity are hidden deep meanings of nature, description, and feeling. Few words are used, so they must be powerful words that describe and show images of nature. It's almost like painting with words.

INTRODUCTORY ACTIVITIES

Before trying to write poetry, students should have many simple opportunities to write creatively. A complete poem is a big project, so young students should achieve success at small creative projects first. They may try changing words of songs, writing endings to songs, or adding accompaniments. Some suggestions below are the early beginnings for creativity and composing music.

1. "Old MacDonald Had a Farm"—Choose animals to fit the song.
2. "If You're Happy and You Know It"—Choose new actions to fit the song.
3. "The Bus Song"—Make up new verses about what happens on a bus.
4. "Here We Go 'Round the Mulberry Bush"—Make up new verses of "This is the way we _____."
5. "She'll Be Coming 'Round the Mountain"—Make up verses about what "we'll do" when she comes.
6. Add rhythmic accompaniments to any song.
7. Go to the bells and make up a phrase or pattern.
8. Make up a song on the black keys of the piano or bells.
9. Draw and color pictures to express listening lessons.
10. Make up a sound story.

COMPOSING AS A CLASS

Review the following rules of Haiku Poetry:

1. Haiku poetry usually deals with nature.
2. Haiku poetry uses descriptive words.
3. The words of Haiku poetry do not have to rhyme.
4. Haiku poetry is composed of three lines with five, seven, and five syllables.

Write three poems on the board to demonstrate these characteristics of Haiku poetry. Use the three given below or find some listed in a poetry book.

September

September starts school,
Laughing, playing, having friends,
Together we work.

Kittens

Soft, fat, furry balls,
Chasing, climbing, frolicking,
Rolling kittens play.

Halloween

Scary black witches
Howling, screeching eerie moans,
Dark night! What a fright!

Choose a subject as a class. This subject should suggest a wide selection of descriptive material (summer, winter, fall, spring, rain, storms, clouds, animals, etc). Once a subject has been chosen, write adjectives on the board. "Winter" will be used for this example. Some words that might be written on the board are:

cold	wonderland
frosty	tracks
glistening	snowman
white	icy
snow	beautiful
fluffy	quiet
bright	peaceful

After adjectives have been listed on the board guide students in arranging some of these adjectives into the proper form of Haiku poetry. Ask "Who can give me five syllables using some of these words that describe winter to begin our poem?" Lead students away from using verbs and making complete sentences. Proceed to the second and third lines of the poem using the same process as for the first line. When the poem is completed it might be similar to the following:

Winter

Glist'ning white winter,
Frosty wonderland glows bright,
Quiet cold beauty.

COMPOSING HAIKU INDIVIDUALLY

After students have tried composing several Haiku poems together on different class days they are ready to attempt writing one by themselves. Hand each student a pencil and piece of paper. List the following steps on the board:

1. Choose a subject. Make sure it has many possibilities for description.
2. List at least ten words that describe the subject.
3. Write the first line of the poem—five syllables.
4. Write the second line of the poem—seven syllables.
5. Write the third line of the poem—five syllables.

Read and display students' efforts in the classroom. Pick out three of the best poems and point out why these are the best (better description, more powerful words, unique idea, better arrangement of words, etc.). Reading and discussing the "best" poems will encourage improvement in future compositions. Do not dismiss *any* efforts, and accept all compositions as good works.

SETTING HAIKU COMPOSITIONS TO MUSIC

The obvious method of setting Haiku poetry to music is use of the pentatonic scale. Not only is it oriental, but it is easy to use, having only five notes. The lack of a tonal center will also simplify the process. Composing melodies should begin as a class project. Choose a poem that the class has written or one of the "best" poems turned in. Have one student come to the bells which have been set up in a pentatonic scale. If bars cannot be removed from bells, ask students to use only the black keys. Have the first student make up a melody for the first line. Students must practice the line until they remember it and can play it the same way every time. The next student comes to the bells and composes a melody for the second line. This will be the most difficult, so choose a student who can handle the task. Finally a third student is chosen to make up the third line melody. Each student who has made up a line of music plays that line. The teacher may want to notate the song and pass it out to students during the next music period. After students compose Haiku poems individually, they may want to compose melodies for them. If only one set of bells is available, place it outside of the classroom. Each student may leave, one at a time, to compose a melody for his or her poem. Students may play them for the class after everyone has finished. It may be necessary to set a time limit, or one student could take up the entire class time. Also, students may forget their compositions by the time they play them for the class. Stress that they must remember the composition to play for the class, so when they're composing, they should keep it simple.

MAY ANSWER KEY

Match the Form

1.	ABAA	6.	ABAA
2.	ABCA	7.	ABBA
3.	ABAB	8.	ABAA
4.	ABCD	9.	AAAB
5.	AABA	10.	ABAB

June

"It's Been a Long Year, but the End Is in Sight"

IT'S BEEN A LONG YEAR, BUT THE END IS IN SIGHT:
The Bulletin Board

Objective: Students will review the concepts learned during the year.

Materials Needed:

Light blue background paper
Construction paper (brown, white, black, red)
Scissors
Straight pins
Glue
Black felt-tip marker

Construction Directions:

1. Use an opaque projector or transparency to trace the letters onto the black construction paper. Cut out and attach the letters to the background with pins.
2. Trace the dog onto brown construction paper with a black marker.
3. Draw the dog's spots on white paper with a black marker. Write the proper words on the spots with a black marker.
4. Cut out all the figures and attach them to the background paper.
5. Fold or bend the dog's head and tail for a three-dimensional effect.
6. You might want to use the red construction paper (instead of black) for the words "LONG" and "END."

IT'S BEEN A LONG YEAR, BUT THE END IS IN SIGHT:
Unit Activities

The final bulletin board features a dachshund with the theme "It's been a long year, but the end is in sight." The dog's spots are labeled with activities and units studied throughout the year. This will serve as a review for the students. At the end of the year, most teachers review and try to tie together things learned during the year. There will be a review of each unit and an activity to test the students' skills and knowledge. Have your students add the dog's spots a few at a time as each concept is reviewed. At the end of the month, the dog should be completed and all activities reviewed.

REVIEW AND TESTS

Blasting Off to a Good Year

If a list of "Good Singing Habits" has been posted somewhere in the room, students can review it frequently. Another final test or review could be to sing the

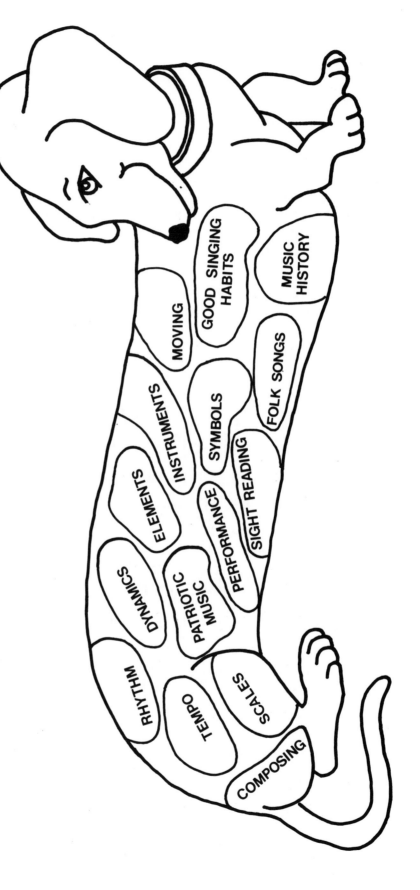

IT'S BEEN A LONG YEAR
BUT THE END IS IN SIGHT

"Good Singing Habits" songs to the tune of "Are You Sleeping?" Younger students may memorize a few of the songs, but older students should know them all by memory.

Let's "Fall" for Music History

This is another bulletin board that could be displayed in the classroom for the entire year. Whenever singing, listening, or studying, students can quickly refer to the period, composer, or form of music. Copies of the "Music History Test" can be given to students as a total review of the information. Younger students may need a simplified version of the test.

Movin' and Groovin'

After reviewing motor skills as presented in the unit, have each class create a routine appropriate to its grade level. Lower grades may take a simple song, such as "Twinkle, Twinkle Little Star," and create actions. Upper grades should create a complete routine to a popular song.

What's Brewing in Music?

The "Music Symbol Test" covers all symbols learned and should only be used for older students. Prepare simpler tests for younger students to be given either at the end of the unit or at the end of the year.

Missing Mystery Instrument

Make copies of the "Instrument Test" and distribute them to your students.

Turkey Tunes

Every class will have a different level of sight-reading ability and should be tested accordingly. Choose rhythm exercises presented in the unit. Next, choose exercises using both rhythms and note values. Finally, select portions of a song or exercises selected from the material presented for testing.

Elves and Elements

Make copies of the "Element Test" and distribute copies to your students.

Star Search

An end-of-the-school-year program is the best way to evaluate performance skills. If a big production is not possible, present a small skit or musical number for individual classrooms. If there is limited time, observe videos of previous programs for students to critique. Use the ten suggestions presented during the unit as a guide.

Chugging into the New Year

The ultimate test of dynamics is for students to use them properly while singing. Students can be tested on how they use dynamics by having them sing the songs at the proper dynamic level. You might also use a familiar song and write various dynamic markings above the words on the chalkboard. Students must observe all markings correctly as a group. Then, change the dynamic markings and see if the students can sing the song properly with the new markings.

Frosty Folk Music

Attitudes are impossible to measure or test, but we need to implement opportunities to develop positive attitudes in our lessons. Folk music, if taught properly, can foster attitudes of pride, just as units on patriotic music promote loyalty and respect for the country. The "Folk Music Test" evaluates your students' knowledge, but only you can deal with their attitudes.

Valentine Values

Make copies of the "Values Test" and distribute copies to your students.

Let's "Ear" It

The final listening test should be a dictation test. Each class will be at a different level, so you will need to follow the unit's suggestions to make appropriate tests for each class. Another final listening project could be to play a recording for one of the worksheets presented in the unit. Students must listen and complete the sheet.

Learning Notes with the Lazy Leprechaun

Make copies of the "Note Name Test" and distribute to your students.

The Tempo Trail

Performance of various tempos is the best testing device. Use songs that are being sung at the end of the school year. Write the words on the chalkboard and fill in various tempo markings. Students should be able to sing the songs correctly. Change the tempo markings of the song several times to evaluate thoroughly.

Showers of Scales

Make copies of the "Scale Test" and distribute them to your students.

Rainbow of Rests

Make copies of the "Rhythm and Rest Test" and distribute them to your students.

Flower Forms

Many tests could be given to evaluate students' knowledge of form. A listening test of "same" and "different," for example, might be presented. Students could also look up songs in their music texts and write the form of the songs, or they could listen to simple four-line songs and write the form of the songs. The ultimate test, however, is to create a song in a certain form (*aba, abc, abac,* etc.). Students must combine a knowledge of composition, rhythms, and notes as well as form to achieve this task. Distribute staff paper that has a particular form at the top, and have students compose according to the form.

Composing with Haiku

Students should compose a final Haiku poem and set it to music. Take a day or two to perform all compositions in class. Students should not judge or criticize the compositions, but simply enjoy the efforts of their fellow classmates.

MUSIC HISTORY TEST

1. Medieval times involved:
   a. castles, kings, and queens
   b. cars, airplanes, and trains
   c. satellites, computers, and spaceships

2. Some medieval Masses were sung in:
   a. sonata
   b. Gregorian chant
   c. variation

3. A "chanson" is a:
   a. stringed instrument
   b. church song
   c. French song

4. Troubadours and trouvères were:
   a. choir directors
   b. traveling performers
   c. fighters

5. A madrigal is:
   a. an Italian love song
   b. a German fighting song
   c. a march

6. *A cappella* means:
   a. singing with instrumental accompaniment
   b. singing without instrumental accompaniment
   c. instruments only

7. Two composers of the medieval period are:
   a. Beethoven and Bach
   b. Mozart and Haydn
   c. Palestrina and Josquin Des Prez

8. *Renaissance* means:
   a. rebirth
   b. old ways
   c. doing again

9. Each variation in a "theme and variations" is:
   a. repeated
   b. omitted
   c. changed

MUSIC HISTORY TEST cont.

10. A canzona is for:
    a. voices only
    b. instruments only
    c. voices and instruments

11. The following might be included in a suite:
    a. minuet and gigue
    b. canzona and cantata
    c. opera and oratorio

12. Composers of the Renaissance are:
    a. Mozart and Haydn
    b. Bartók and Tchaikovsky
    c. Byrd and Morley

13. The Baroque period marks a:
    a. fancy and ornamental time
    b. simplified time
    c. back-to-the-basics time

14. A fugue is:
    a. homophonic
    b. polyphonic
    c. monophonic

15. The master of fugue is:
    a. Bach
    b. Beethoven
    c. Mozart

16. Preludes are often performed:
    a. before church services
    b. after weddings
    c. at political rallies

17. A cantata would most likely be performed:
    a. at a funeral
    b. at a wedding
    c. at a church service

18. The music of the Classical period is:
    a. made up of modal harmony
    b. refined and elegant
    c. extremely fancy and ornamental

MUSIC HISTORY TEST cont.

19. Songs in opera are called:
    a. arias
    b. recitatives
    c. sonatas

20. A sonata usually features:
    a. a band
    b. an orchestra
    c. a solo instrument

21. Symphonies are played by:
    a. a solo instrument
    b. an orchestra
    c. a small ensemble

22. Two composers of the Classical period are:
    a. Mozart and Haydn
    b. Palestrina and Josquin Des Pres
    c. Bartók and Stravinsky

23. The Romantic period is best described by the word:
    a. emotionalism
    b. simplicity
    c. ornamental

24. The string quartet uses:
    a. four violins
    b. four cellos
    c. two violins, a viola, and a cello

25. The composer who bridged the Classical and Romantic periods is:
    a. Beethoven
    b. Bach
    c. Bartók

26. The new avenue of twentieth-century music is:
    a. electronics
    b. stringed instruments
    c. brass instruments

27. The development of the tone row came from:
    a. Bartók
    b. Ravel
    c. Schoenberg

MUSIC HISTORY TEST cont.

28. Pop music originated from:
    a. electronic music
    b. jazz
    c. chance music

29. Two composers of the twentieth century are:
    a. Mozart and Haydn
    b. Ives and Bartók
    c. Palestrina and Josquin Des Prez

30. The total number of periods in music history studied this year is:
    a. two
    b. four
    c. six

MUSIC SYMBOL TEST

PART ONE: Read each statement and decide whether it's true or false. Write a "T" for true or an "F" for false.

_____ 1.   c or common time is 4/4 time.

_____ 2.   The symbol for medium loud is "mf."

_____ 3.   The symbol for very loud is "f."

_____ 4.   The bass clef is usually played by low instruments.

_____ 5.   A tie and a slur are the same thing.

_____ 6.   A natural sign can cancel sharps but not flats.

_____ 7.   The top number in a time signature tells what kind of note gets one count.

_____ 8.   Accents make the notes louder.

_____ 9.   Sharps lower notes by a half step.

_____ 10.   Double bar lines occur at the end of songs.

PART TWO: Draw the following symbols.

1.   Treble clef   _____

2.   Crescendo sign   _____

3.   Flat   _____

4.   Cut time   _____

5.   Bass clef   _____

6.   Repeat sign   _____

7.   Letters for "very soft"   _____

8.   Time signature with two counts in a measure and the quarter note getting one count   _____

9.   Double bar line   _____

10.   Whole note   _____

Name _____ Date _____

INSTRUMENT TEST

Complete each statement with the correct answer.

1. A _____ is an electronic instrument that can make many sounds.

2. The _____ family includes instruments that you can either hit or shake to play.

3. Another name for a violin is a _____.

4. The _____ plays the bird in *Peter and the Wolf.*

5. Two families of instruments that are blown are _____ and _____.

6. The _____ and viola are very similar.

7. Chopin's major instrument was the _____.

8. The piano has _____ keys.

9. Name four brass family instruments:

   _____   _____

   _____   _____

10. The _____ is used to tune the orchestra.

11. Orchestras are mainly made up of instruments from the _____ family.

12. Bands do not have any instruments from the _____ family.

13. A fife is like a _____.

14. An ancient instrument that resembles the guitar is a _____.

15. A brass instrument with a slide is a _____.

Name _____   **Date** _____

ELEMENT TEST

1. Name the five elements of music:

   _____

   _____

   _____

   _____

   _____

2. _____ go up, down, or stay the same.

3. Oriental melodies are based on _____ scales.

4. Write a melody on the following staff:

   _____
   _____
   _____
   _____
   _____

5. Draw four quarter notes and two half notes: _____

6. Write the counts under these measures:

7. Notate the following names:
   Nancy King   Burt Howard   Melissa Crosby

8. Name the four families of instruments:

   _____

   _____

   _____

   _____

9. Name an instrument you might use to portray each of the following animals:

   bird _____   elephant _____

   cat _____   horse _____

10. In music, form is shown by _____.

11. Listen to the examples your teacher will clap. Each set of rhythms may be either the SAME or DIFFERENT. Write "S" for same, and a "D" for different.

    a. _____   d. _____

    b. _____   e. _____

    c. _____

ELEMENT TEST cont.

12. What is the form of "Twinkle, Twinkle Little Star"? _____

13. Sad songs use _____ harmonies.

14. The three chords most often used to harmonize are _____, _____, and _____.

15. Write two chords on the staff below:

FOLK MUSIC TEST

1. The following song came from England:
   a. "Pop Goes the Weasel"
   b. "Oh, Susanna"
   c. "Down the River"

2. "Pop Goes the Weasel" is about:
   a. two animals
   b. a tailor's machine
   c. two people

3. Sea songs are called:
   a. ballads
   b. serenades
   c. chanties

4. Work songs were sung:
   a. very fast
   b. in the rhythm of the work
   c. very slowly

5. Spirituals are:
   a. religious
   b. funny
   c. marches

6. "Yankee Doodle" was sung:
   a. during the Civil War
   b. during World War II
   c. during the Revolutionary War

7. The president mentioned in "Yankee Doodle" is:
   a. George Washington
   b. Thomas Jefferson
   c. Abraham Lincoln

8. "Yankee Doodle" was written to make fun of the:
   a. British
   b. Germans
   c. Americans

FOLK MUSIC TEST cont.

9. The musical instruments carried into battle during the Revolutionary War were:

   a. trumpets and trombones

   b. fifes and drums

   c. flutes and saxophones

10. The tarriers in "Drill Ye Tarriers" are:

    a. dogs

    b. cowboys

    c. railroad workers

11. "Sweet Betsy from Pike" is a song about:

    a. gold mining

    b. going west

    c. dancing

12. "Home on the Range" is a song of the:

    a. cowboy

    b. sailor

    c. railroad worker

13. Rivers provide a great means of:

    a. transportation

    b. cowboys

    c. food

14. "Hop Up My Ladies" and "Skip to My Lou" were sung by the settlers at:

    a. churches

    b. meetings

    c. funerals

15. Folk songs are a part of our:

    a. heritage

    b. present life

    c. responsibility

Name _____ **Date** _____

VALUES TEST

1. Two whole notes equal _____ quarter notes.

2. Draw a half note and two quarter notes: _____

3. A dot adds _____ of the note's value.

4. It takes _____ eighth notes to make a half note.

5. Draw a sixteenth note: _____

6. Draw the time signature with three counts to a measure and a quarter note getting one count: _____

7. Add these problems if the time signature is $\frac{?}{4}$:

   a. ♩ + ♩ + ♩ + 𝅝 =

   b. ♫ + ♩ + ♩. + 𝅗𝅥 =

   c. ♩ + ♩ + ♩ + ♪ =

8. Draw in the bar lines at the proper places:

9. Write the correct counts under the notes:

VALUES TEST cont.

10.   Fill in the time signatures:

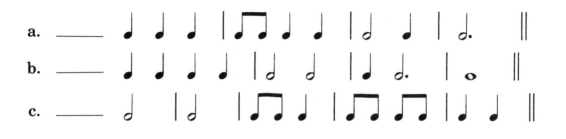

a. _____

b. _____

c. _____

NOTE NAME TEST

PART ONE: Write in the names of the notes:

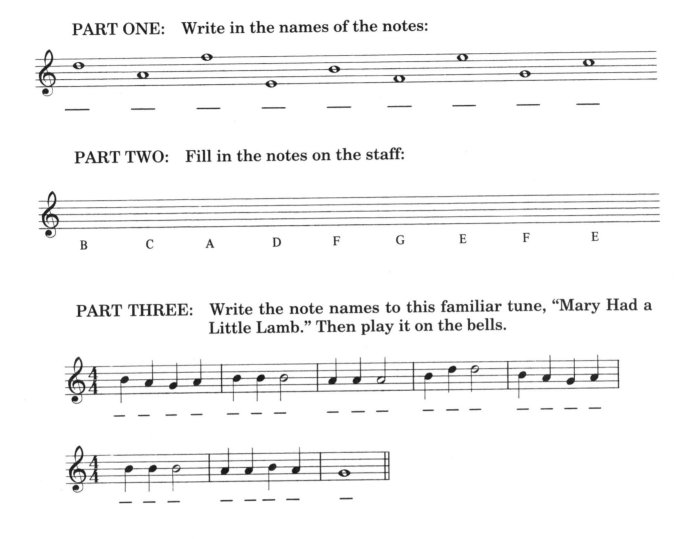

PART TWO: Fill in the notes on the staff:

B   C   A   D   F   G   E   F   E

PART THREE: Write the note names to this familiar tune, "Mary Had a Little Lamb." Then play it on the bells.

SCALE TEST

Using the formula of whole and half steps (WWHWWWH), write the following scales on the staffs.

D Scale

F Scale

Play the following scales:
a. C Major
b. A minor
c. Pentatonic
d. Chromatic

Name_____ **Date**_____

RHYTHM AND REST TEST

PART ONE: Write the appropriate rest for each rhythm.

1. 𝅝 =   4. ♪ =

2. 𝅗𝅥 =   5. ♪ =

3. ♩ =

PART TWO: Complete each measure with rests. For some of the measures, there may be more than one correct answer.

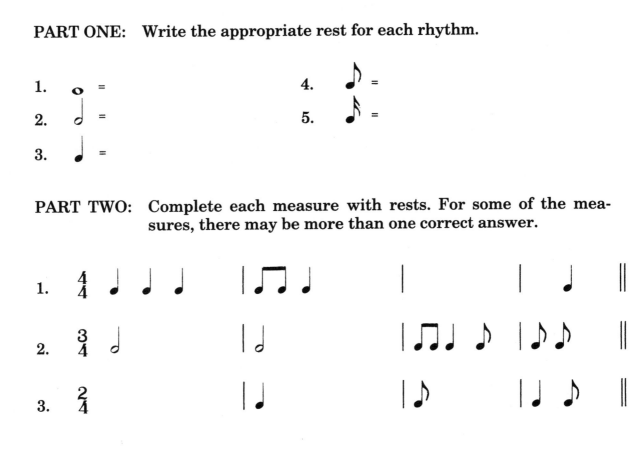

PART THREE: Add the following rests using a time signature in which a quarter note gets one count.

1. 𝄽 + 𝄽 + 𝄻 =

2. 𝄾 + 𝄾 + 𝄾 + 𝄾 =

3. 𝄻 + 𝄻 + 𝄻 =

4. 𝄽 + 𝄽 + 𝄻 =

5. 𝄾 + 𝄾 + 𝄾 + 𝄽 =

PART FOUR: Write a rhythm composition of four measures using at least two rests. Then play the composition.

JUNE ANSWER KEY

Music History Test

1.	a	11.	a	21.	b
2.	b	12.	c	22.	a
3.	c	13.	a	23.	a
4.	b	14.	b	24.	c
5.	a	15.	a	25.	a
6.	b	16.	a	26.	a
7.	c	17.	c	27.	c
8.	a	18.	b	28.	b
9.	c	19.	a	29.	b
10.	b	20.	a	30.	c

Music Symbol Test

Part One:

1.	T	6.	F
2.	T	7.	F
3.	F	8.	T
4.	T	9.	F
5.	F	10.	T

Part Two:

1. (treble clef)
2. (crescendo symbol)
3. (flat symbol)
4. (cut time symbol)
5. (bass clef)

6. (repeat sign)
7. *pp*
8. $\frac{2}{4}$
9. (double bar line)
10. (whole note)

Instrument Test

1. synthesizer
2. percussion
3. fiddle
4. flute
5. brass, woodwind
6. violin
7. piano
8. 88
9. trumpet, trombone, French horn, tuba, cornet, etc.
10. oboe
11. string
12. string
13. flute
14. lute
15. trombone

Element Test

1. melody, harmony, rhythm, form, tone color
2. melodies
3. pentatonic
4. Answers will vary

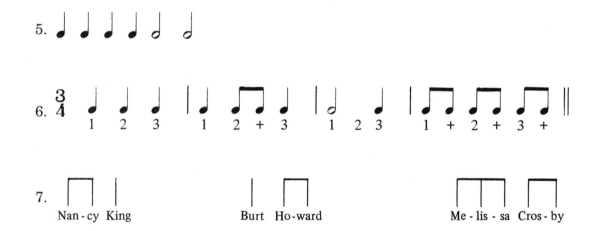

5.

6.

7. Nan-cy King   Burt Ho-ward   Me-lis-sa Cros-by

8. strings, brass, woodwinds, percussion
9. Answers will vary
10. Letters, ABC, etc.
11. Answers will vary
12. ABA
13. minor
14. I, IV, V
15. Answers will vary

Folk Music Test

1.	a	6.	c	11.	b
2.	b	7.	a	12.	a
3.	c	8.	c	13.	a
4.	b	9.	b	14.	b
5.	a	10.	c	15.	a, b, c

Values Test

1. 8

2.

3. one-half

4. 4

5.

6. $\frac{3}{4}$

7. a. = 8

    b. = 7

    c. = 4½

8. a.

    b.

    c.

9. a.

10. a. $\dfrac{3}{4}$

b. $\dfrac{4}{4}$

c. $\dfrac{2}{4}$

Note Name Test

Part One: D A F E B F E G C

Part Two:

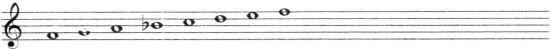

Part Three: B A G A B B B A A A B D D B A G A B B B A A B A G

Scale Test

D Scale:

F Scale:

Rhythm and Rest Test

Part One:

1. ▬
2. ▬
3. 𝄽
4. 𝄾
5. 𝄿

Part Two: Answers will vary. Some possibilities are given below.

1. $\frac{4}{4}$ ♩ ♩ ♩ 𝄽 | ♫ ♩ ▬ | ▬ | ♩ 𝄽 𝄽 𝄽 ‖

2. $\frac{3}{4}$ ♩ 𝄽 𝄽 | ♩ 𝄽 | ♫ ♩ ♪𝄿 | ♪ ♪ 𝄽 𝄽 ‖

3. $\frac{2}{4}$ 𝄽 𝄽 | ♩ 𝄽 | ♪𝄿 𝄽 | ♩ ♪𝄿 ‖

Part Three:

1. 𝄾 + 𝄽 + ▬ = 5½

2. 𝄾 + 𝄿 + 𝄿 + 𝄿 = 1¼

3. ▬ + ▬ + ▬ = 8

4. 𝄽 + 𝄽 + ▬ = 6

5. 𝄾 + 𝄿 + 𝄿 + 𝄽 = 2

Part Four: Answers will vary.

RESOURCES FOR ADDITIONAL INFORMATION

CHORAL TECHNIQUES AND PERFORMANCE

Harpster, Richard W. *Technique in Singing* (New York: Schirmer Books, 1984).

Kohut, Daniel L. *Musical Performance* (Englewood Cliffs, NJ: Prentice-Hall, 1985).

Miller, Richard. *The Structure of Singing* (New York: Schirmer Books, 1986).

Swears, Linda. *Teaching the Elementary School Chorus* (West Nyack, NY: Parker Publishing Company, 1985).

Van Camp, Leonard. *Choral Warm-Ups* (New York: Lawson-Gould, 1972).

Weil, Paul and Esther. *First Steps in Part Singing* (New York: G. Schirmer, 1968).

EAR TRAINING

Benward, Bruce. *Ear Training* (Dubuque, IA: Wm. C. Brown Publishing, 1978).

Evans, Dr. George K. *Bowmar Orchestral Library*, record set (Oklahoma City: Bowmar-Noble, 1967).

Levy, Kenneth. *Music, A Listener's Introduction* (New York: Harper and Row, 1983).

Mack, Floyd. *Pathways to Music* (New York: Keyboard Publications, 1978).

McGaughey, Janet McCloud. *Practical Ear Training* (New York: Crescendo Publications, 1970).

Tipton, Gladys, and Eleanor Tipton. *Adventures in Music*, record set (New York: RCA, 1962).

ELEMENTS OF MUSIC

Adler, Marvin S., and Jesse C. McCarroll. *Making Music Fun* (West Nyack, NY: Parker Publishing Company, 1970).

Gordon, Edwin E. *Learning Sequence and Patterns in Music* (Chicago: GIA Publications, 1977).

Levy, Ernest. *A Theory of Harmony* (New York: State University of New York Press, 1985).

Makas, Dr. George. "Hello, I'm Music" film set (St. Paul, MN: EMC Publishing, 1969).

Nye, Robert Evans, and Vernice Trousdale Nye. *Music in the Elementary School* (Englewood Cliffs, NJ: Prentice-Hall, 1985).

Orff-Schulwerk. *Music for Children*, American Edition (New York: Schott Music Corporation, 1977).

Ottman, Robert W. *Elementary Harmony* (Englewood Cliffs, NJ: Prentice-Hall, 1983).

Tovey, Donald Francis. *Forms of Music* (New York: Meridian Books, 1959).

Williams, Martin. *Where's the Melody?* (New York: Pantheon Books, 1966).

FOLK SONGS

Chase, Gilbert. *America's Music* (New York: McGraw-Hill, 1968).

Diton, Carl. *Thirty-six South Carolina Spirituals* (New York: G. Schirmer, 1930).

Krehbiel, Henry Edward. *Afro-American Folk Songs* (New York: Fredric Ungar Publishing, 1975).

Leach, Robert, and Roy Palmer. *Folk Music in School* (London: Cambridge University Press, 1978).

Lingenfelter, Richard, Richard A. Dwyer, and David Cohen. *Songs of the American West* (Berkeley: University Press of California, 1968).

Lomax, Alan. *Folk Songs of North America* (New York: Doubleday and Company, 1960).

Nettl, Bruno. *Folk Music in the United States* (Detroit: Wayne State University Press, 1976).

Nordeff, Paul. *Folk Songs for Children to Sing and Play* (Bryn Mawr, PA: Theodore Presser Co., 1977).

Sandberg, Larry, and Dick Weissman. *The Folk Music Sourcebook* (New York: Alfred A. Knopf Publishing, 1976).

Seeger, Ruth Crawford. *American Folk Songs for Children* (New York: Doubleday and Company, 1948).

INSTRUMENTS IN MUSIC

Apel, Willi. *The History of Keyboard Music* (Bloomington: Indiana University Press, 1972).

The Diagram Group. *Orchestral Instruments* (New York: Charles Scribner's and Sons, 1983).

Dodge, Charles, and Thomas A. Jerse. *Computer Music* (New York: G. Schirmer, 1977).

Dorf, Richard. *Electronic Musical Instruments* (New York: Plimpton Press, 1968).

Ernst, David. *Evolution of Electronic Music* (New York: G. Schirmer, 1977).

Remnant, Mary. *Music Instruments of the West* (New York: St. Martin's Press, 1978).

Sawyer, David. *Vibrations—Making Unorthodox Musical Instruments* (London: Cambridge University Press, 1977).

Singleton, Esther. *The Orchestra and Its Instruments* (New York: The Symphony Society, 1920).

Stewart, Madeau. *The Music Lover's Guide to Instruments of the Orchestra* (New York: Van Nostrand Reinhold, 1980).

Wood, Lucille. *Meet the Instruments* (Oklahoma City: Bowmar-Noble, 1961).

MOVEMENT AND DANCE

Albrecht, Sally K. *Choral Music in Motion* (Stroudsburg, PA: Music in Action, 1980).

Burnett, Millie. *Melody, Movement, and Language* (Allison Park, PA: Musik Innovations, 1973).

Findlay, Elsa. *Rhythm and Movement* (Evanston, IL: Summy-Birchard Co., 1971).

Gelineau, R. Phyllis. *Songs in Action, Second Edition* (West Nyack, NY: Parker Publishing Company, 1988).

Haselbach, Barbara. *Improvisation, Dance, and Movement*, translated by Margaret Murray (St. Louis: MMB Music, 1981).

Lucky, Sharron. *Rhythm and Rhyme* (Oklahoma City: Melody House Publishing, 1979).

Nelson, Esther. *Movement Games for Children of All Ages* (New York: Sterling Publishing, 1975).

Shotwell, Rita. *Rhythm and Movement Activities* (Port Washington, NY: Alfred Publishing, 1974).

MUSIC HISTORY

Baker, Theodore. *Baker's Biographical Dictionary of Musicians* (New York: G. Schirmer, 1977).

Ewen, David. *Composers of Yesterday* (New York: H. W. Wilson, 1977).

Finny, Theodore M. *A History of Music* (Westport, CT: Greenwood Press, 1975).

Grout, Jay. *A History of Western Music* (New York: W. W. Norton and Co., 1980).

Harman, Alec, Wilfred Mellers, and Anthony Herman. *Man and His Music* (New York: Oxford University Press, 1962).

SIGHT SINGING AND NOTE READING

Arkis, Stanley, and Herman Shuckman. *An Introduction to Sight Singing* (New York: Carl Fischer, 1969).

Chosky, Lois. *The Kodály Context* (Englewood Cliffs, NJ: Prentice-Hall, 1981).

Harrison, Lois. *Getting Started in Elementary Music Education* (Englewood Cliffs, NJ: Prentice-Hall, 1983).

Kliewer, Vernon L. *Music Reading* (Englewood Cliffs, NJ: Prentice-Hall, 1973).

Schaum, John. *Theory Lessons* (Melville, NY: Belwin-Mills, 1946).

Scipiades, Katinka. *Kodály in Kindergarten* (Champaign, IL: Daniel Mark Foster Publications, 1981).

Vandre, Carl. *Part Sight Reading Fun* (Melville, NY: Belwin-Mills, 1968).

Wheeler, Lawrence, and Lois Raebeck. *Orff and Kodály Adapted for the Elementary School* (Dubuque, IA: Wm. C. Brown Co., 1972).

Williams, C. F. Abdy. *The Story of Notation* (Westport, CT: Greenwood Press, 1969).

Woskowiak, Leona Frances. *Programmed Music Reading Games for First Grade* (University Park: Pennsylvania State University Press, 1973).

Wright, Don. *It's Fun to Read Music* (New York: Robbins Music Corporation, 1970).

RHYTHM IN MUSIC

Findlay, Elsa. *Rhythm and Movement* (Evanston, IL: Summy-Birchard Co., 1971).

Jaques-Dalcroze, Emile. *Rhythm, Music and Education*, translated by Harold F. Rubinstein (Salem, NH: Arno Press, 1976).

Nash, Grace. *Music with Children: Rhythmic Speech Ensembles* (LaGrange, IL: Kitching Education, 1970).

Sacho, Curt. *Rhythm and Tempo* (New York: W. W. Norton, 1953).

Schaum, Wesley. *Rhythm Workbook* (Milwaukee: Schaum Publishing, 1969).

Winick, Steven. *Rhythm* (Metuchen, NJ: Scarecrow Press, 1974).

TEACHING MUSIC AND THEORY

Athey, Margaret, and Gwen Hotchkiss. *Treasury of Individualized Activities for the Music Class* (West Nyack, NY: Parker Publishing Company, 1977).

Barnes, Robert A. *Fundamentals of Music* (New York: McGraw-Hill, 1964).

Baur, John. *Music Theory Through Literature* (Englewood Cliffs, NJ: Prentice-Hall, 1985).

Choksy, Lois, Robert M. Abramson, Aaron E. Gillespie, and David Woods. *Teaching Music in the Twentieth Century* (Englewood Cliffs, NJ: Prentice-Hall, 1986).

Forquer, Nancy. *Elementary Teacher's Complete Handbook of Music Activities* (West Nyack, NY: Parker Publishing Company, 1979).

Grant, Parks. *Music for the Elementary Teacher* (New York: Appleton-Century-Crofts, 1960).

Marsh, Mary Val. *Explore and Discover Music* (New York/London: The Macmillan Co., 1970).

Reynolds, Jane. *Music Lessons You Can Teach* (West Nyack, NY: Parker Publishing Company, 1981).

Rothman, Joel. *Easy Music Crossword Puzzles* (Ft. Lauderdale, FL: J. R. Publications, 1984).